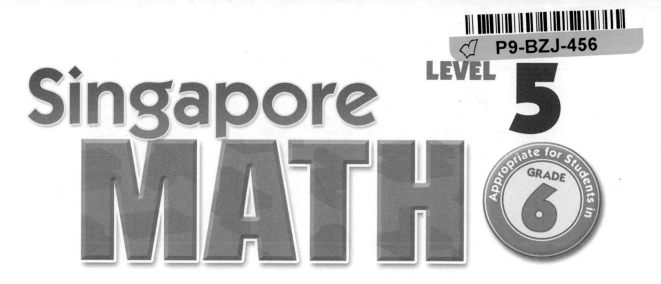

Singapore MATH

LEVEL **5**

Appropriate for Students in GRADE **6**

P9-BZJ-456

70 Must-Know WORD PROBLEMS

Frank Schaffer
An imprint of Carson-Dellosa Publishing LLC
Greensboro, North Carolina

Copyright © 2009 Singapore Asian Publications (S) Pte. Ltd.

Frank Schaffer
An imprint of Carson-Dellosa Publishing LLC
PO Box 35665
Greensboro, NC 27425 USA

Printed in the USA • All rights reserved.
3 4 5 6 GLO 13 12 11 10

ISBN 978-0-7682-4015-3
245107784

INTRODUCTION TO SINGAPORE MATH

Welcome to Singapore Math! The math curriculum in Singapore has been recognized worldwide for its excellence In producing students highly skilled in mathematics. Students in Singapore have ranked at the top in the world in mathematics on the *Trends in International Mathematics and Science Study* (TIMSS) in 1993, 1995, 2003, and 2008. Because of this, Singapore Math has gained in interest and popularity in the United States.

Singapore Math curriculum aims to help students develop the necessary math concepts and process skills for everyday life and to provide students with the ability to formulate, apply, and solve problems. Mathematics in the Singapore Primary (Elementary) Curriculum cover fewer topics but in greater depth. Key math concepts are introduced and built-on to reinforce various mathematical ideas and thinking. Students in Singapore are typically one grade level ahead of students in the United States.

The following pages provide examples of the various math problem types and skill sets taught in Singapore.

At an elementary level, some simple mathematical skills can help students understand mathematical principles. These skills are the counting-on, counting-back, and crossing-out methods. Note that these methods are most useful when the numbers are small.

1. The Counting-On Method

Used for addition of two numbers. Count on in 1s with the help of a picture or number line.

$$7 + 4 = \mathbf{11}$$

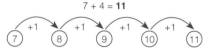

2. The Counting-Back Method

Used for subtraction of two numbers. Count back in 1s with the help of a picture or number line.

$$16 - 3 = \mathbf{13}$$

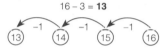

3. The Crossing-Out Method

Used for subtraction of two numbers. Cross out the number of items to be taken away. Count the remaining ones to find the answer.

$$20 - 12 = \mathbf{8}$$

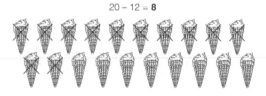

A **number bond** shows the relationship in a simple addition or subtraction problem. The number bond is based on the concept "part-part-whole." This concept is useful in teaching simple addition and subtraction to young children.

To find a whole, students must add the two parts.
To find a part, students must subtract the other part from the whole.

The different types of number bonds are illustrated below.

1. Number Bond (single digits)

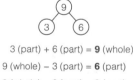

$$3 \text{ (part)} + 6 \text{ (part)} = \mathbf{9} \text{ (whole)}$$
$$9 \text{ (whole)} - 3 \text{ (part)} = \mathbf{6} \text{ (part)}$$
$$9 \text{ (whole)} - 6 \text{ (part)} = \mathbf{3} \text{ (part)}$$

2. Addition Number Bond (single digits)

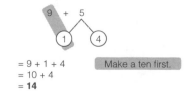

$$= 9 + 1 + 4$$
$$= 10 + 4$$
$$= \mathbf{14}$$

| Make a ten first. |

3. Addition Number Bond (double and single digits)

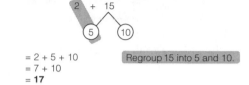

$$= 2 + 5 + 10$$
$$= 7 + 10$$
$$= \mathbf{17}$$

| Regroup 15 into 5 and 10. |

4. Subtraction Number Bond (double and single digits)

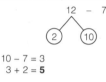

$$10 - 7 = 3$$
$$3 + 2 = \mathbf{5}$$

5. Subtraction Number Bond (double digits)

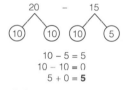

$$10 - 5 = 5$$
$$10 - 10 = 0$$
$$5 + 0 = \mathbf{5}$$

Students should understand that multiplication is repeated addition and that division is the grouping of all items into equal sets.

1. Repeated Addition (Multiplication)

Mackenzie eats 2 rolls a day. How many rolls does she eat in 5 days?

$$2 + 2 + 2 + 2 + 2 = 10$$
$$5 \times 2 = 10$$

She eats **10** rolls in 5 days.

2. The Grouping Method (Division)

Mrs. Lee makes 14 sandwiches. She gives all the sandwiches equally to 7 friends. How many sandwiches does each friend receive?

$$14 \div 7 = 2$$

Each friend receives **2** sandwiches.

One of the basic but essential math skills students should acquire is to perform the 4 operations of whole numbers and fractions. Each of these methods is illustrated below.

1. The Adding-Without-Regrouping Method

```
  H T O
  3 2 1        O: Ones
+ 5 6 8        T: Tens
-------
  8 8 9        H: Hundreds
```

Since no regrouping is required, add the digits in each place value accordingly.

2. The Adding-by-Regrouping Method

```
  H T O
 ¹4 9 2        O: Ones
+ 1 5 3        T: Tens
-------
  6 4 5        H: Hundreds
```

In this example, regroup 14 tens into 1 hundred 4 tens.

3. The Adding-by-Regrouping-Twice Method

```
  H  T  O
 ¹2 ¹8  6        O: Ones
+  3  6  5       T: Tens
 ─────────       H: Hundreds
  6  5  1
```

Regroup twice in this example.
First, regroup 11 ones into 1 ten 1 one.
Second, regroup 15 tens into 1 hundred 5 tens.

4. The Subtracting-Without-Regrouping Method

```
  H  T  O
  7  3  9        O: Ones
−  3  2  5       T: Tens
 ─────────       H: Hundreds
  4  1  4
```

Since no regrouping is required, subtract the digits in each place value accordingly.

5. The Subtracting-by-Regrouping Method

```
  H  T  O
  5 ⁷8 ¹¹1       O: Ones
−  2  4  7       T: Tens
 ─────────       H: Hundreds
  3  3  4
```

In this example, students cannot subtract 7 ones from 1 one. So, regroup the tens and ones. Regroup 8 tens 1 one into 7 tens 11 ones.

6. The Subtracting-by-Regrouping-Twice Method

```
   H  T  O
  ⁷8 ⁹0 ¹⁰0      O: Ones
−  5  9  3       T: Tens
 ──────────      H: Hundreds
   2  0  7
```

In this example, students cannot subtract 3 ones from 0 ones and 9 tens from 0 tens. So, regroup the hundreds, tens, and ones. Regroup 8 hundreds into 7 hundreds 9 tens 10 ones.

7. The Multiplying-Without-Regrouping Method

```
   T  O
   2  4          O: Ones
×     2          T: Tens
 ───────
   4  8
```

Since no regrouping is required, multiply the digit in each place value by the multiplier accordingly.

8. The Multiplying-With-Regrouping Method

```
   H  T  O
  ¹3 ²4  9       O: Ones
×        3       T: Tens
 ──────────      H: Hundreds
 1, 0  4  7
```

In this example, regroup 27 ones into 2 tens 7 ones, and 14 tens into 1 hundred 4 tens.

9. The Dividing-Without-Regrouping Method

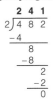

```
      2  4  1
   2)  4  8  2
      −4
      ──
       8
      −8
      ──
       2
      −2
      ──
       0
```

Since no regrouping is required, divide the digit in each place value by the divisor accordingly.

10. The Dividing-With-Regrouping Method

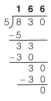

```
      1  6  6
   5)  8  3  0
      −5
      ──
       3  3
      −3  0
      ────
          3  0
         −3  0
         ────
             0
```

In this example, regroup 3 hundreds into 30 tens and add 3 tens to make 33 tens. Regroup 3 tens into 30 ones.

11. The Addition-of-Fractions Method

$$\frac{1}{6} \times 2 + \frac{1}{4} \times 3 = \frac{2}{12} + \frac{3}{12} = \frac{5}{12}$$

Always remember to make the denominators common before adding the fractions.

12. The Subtraction-of-Fractions Method

$$\frac{1}{2} \times 5 - \frac{1}{5} \times 2 = \frac{5}{10} - \frac{2}{10} = \frac{3}{10}$$

Always remembers to make the denominators common before subtracting the fractions.

13. The Multiplication-of-Fractions Method

$$\frac{1\cancel{3}}{5} \times \frac{1}{\cancel{3}9} = \frac{1}{15}$$

When the numerator and the denominator have a common multiple, reduce them to their lowest fractions.

14. The Division-of-Fractions Method

$$\frac{7}{9} \div \frac{1}{6} = \frac{7}{\cancel{9}3} \times \frac{\cancel{6}2}{1} = \frac{14}{3} = 4\frac{2}{3}$$

When dividing fractions, first change the division sign (÷) to the multiplication sign (×). Then, switch the numerator and denominator of the fraction on the right hand side. Multiply the fractions in the usual way.

Model drawing is an effective strategy used to solve math word problems. It is a visual representation of the information in word problems using bar units. By drawing the models, students will know of the variables given in the problem, the variables to find, and even the methods used to solve the problem.

Drawing models is also a versatile strategy. It can be applied to simple word problems involving addition, subtraction, multiplication, and division. It can also be applied to word problems related to fractions, decimals, percentage, and ratio.

The use of models also trains students to think in an algebraic manner, which uses symbols for representation.

The different types of bar models used to solve word problems are illustrated below.

1. The model that involves addition

Melissa has 50 blue beads and 20 red beads. How many beads does she have altogether?

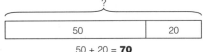

$50 + 20 = \textbf{70}$

2. The model that involves subtraction

Ben and Andy have 90 toy cars. Andy has 60 toy cars. How many toy cars does Ben have?

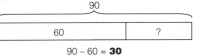

$90 - 60 = \textbf{30}$

3. The model that involves comparison

Mr. Simons has 150 magazines and 110 books in his study. How many more magazines than books does he have?

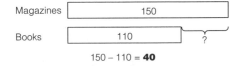

$150 - 110 = \textbf{40}$

4. The model that involves two items with a difference

A pair of shoes costs $109. A leather bag costs $241 more than the pair of shoes. How much is the leather bag?

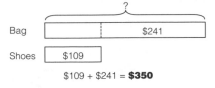

$109 + $241 = \textbf{\$350}$

5. The model that involves multiples

Mrs. Drew buys 12 apples. She buys 3 times as many oranges as apples. She also buys 3 times as many cherries as oranges. How many pieces of fruit does she buy altogether?

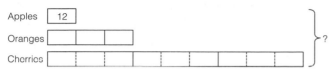

$$13 \times 12 = \textbf{156}$$

6. The model that involves multiples and difference

There are 15 students in Class A. There are 5 more students in Class B than in Class A. There are 3 times as many students in Class C than in Class A. How many students are there altogether in the three classes?

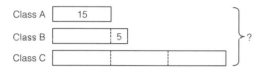

$$(5 \times 15) + 5 = \textbf{80}$$

7. The model that involves creating a whole

Ellen, Giselle, and Brenda bake 111 muffins. Giselle bakes twice as many muffins as Brenda. Ellen bakes 9 fewer muffins than Giselle. How many muffins does Ellen bake?

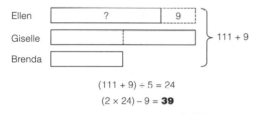

$$(111 + 9) \div 5 = 24$$
$$(2 \times 24) - 9 = \textbf{39}$$

8. The model that involves sharing

There are 183 tennis balls in Basket A and 97 tennis balls in Basket B. How many tennis balls must be transferred from Basket A to Basket B so that both baskets contain the same number of tennis balls?

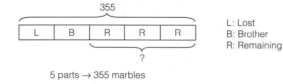

$$183 - 97 = 86$$
$$86 \div 2 = \textbf{43}$$

9. The model that involves fractions

George had 355 marbles. He lost $\frac{1}{5}$ of the marbles and gave $\frac{1}{4}$ of the remaining marbles to his brother. How many marbles did he have left?

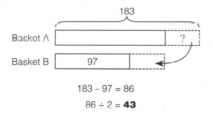

L: Lost
B: Brother
R: Remaining

5 parts → 355 marbles
1 part → 355 ÷ 5 = 71 marbles
3 parts → 3 × 71 = **213** marbles

10. The model that involves ratio

Aaron buys a tie and a belt. The prices of the tie and belt are in the ratio 2 : 5. If both items cost $539,

(a) what is the price of the tie?

(b) what is the price of the belt?

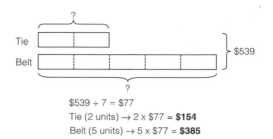

$$\$539 \div 7 = \$77$$
Tie (2 units) → 2 × $77 = **$154**
Belt (5 units) → 5 × $77 = **$385**

11. The model that involves comparison of fractions

Jack's height is $\frac{2}{3}$ of Leslie's height. Leslie's height is $\frac{3}{4}$ of Lindsay's height. If Lindsay is 160 cm tall, find Jack's height and Leslie's height.

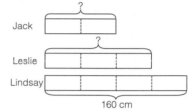

1 unit → 160 ÷ 4 = 40 cm

Leslie's height (3 units) → 3 × 40 = **120 cm**

Jack's height (2 units) → 2 × 40 = **80 cm**

Thinking skills and strategies are important in mathematical problem solving. These skills are applied when students think through the math problems to solve them. Below are some commonly used thinking skills and strategies applied in mathematical problem solving.

1. Comparing

Comparing is a form of thinking skill that students can apply to identify similarities and differences.

When comparing numbers, look carefully at each digit before deciding if a number is greater or less than the other. Students might also use a number line for comparison when there are more numbers.

Example:

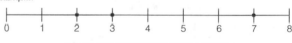

3 is greater than 2 but smaller than 7.

2. Sequencing

A sequence shows the order of a series of numbers. *Sequencing* is a form of thinking skill that requires students to place numbers in a particular order. There are many terms in a sequence. The terms refer to the numbers in a sequence.

To place numbers in a correct order, students must first find a rule that generates the sequence. In a simple math sequence, students can either add or subtract to find the unknown terms in the sequence.

Example: Find the 7th term in the sequence below.

1,	4,	7,	10,	13,	16	?
1st term	2nd term	3rd term	4th term	5th term	6th term	7th term

Step 1: This sequence is in an increasing order.

Step 2: 4 − 1 = 3   7 − 4 = 3
The difference between two consecutive terms is 3.

Step 3: 16 + 3 = 19
The 7th term is **19**.

3. Visualization

Visualization is a problem solving strategy that can help students visualize a problem through the use of physical objects. Students will play a more active role in solving the problem by manipulating these objects.

The main advantage of using this strategy is the mobility of information in the process of solving the problem. When students make a wrong step in the process, they can retrace the step without erasing or canceling it.

The other advantage is that this strategy helps develop a better understanding of the problem or solution through visual objects or images. In this way, students will be better able to remember how to solve these types of problems.

Some of the commonly used objects for this strategy are toothpicks, straws, cards, strings, water, sand, pencils, paper, and dice.

4. Look for a Pattern

This strategy requires the use of observational and analytical skills. Students have to observe the given data to find a pattern in order to solve the problem. Math word problems that involve the use of this strategy usually have repeated numbers or patterns.

Example: Find the sum of all the numbers from 1 to 100.

Step 1: Simplify the problem.

Find the sum of 1, 2, 3, 4, 5, 6, 7, 8, 9, and 10.

Step 2: Look for a pattern.

$1 + 10 = 11$ $2 + 9 = 11$ $3 + 8 = 11$
$4 + 7 = 11$ $5 + 6 = 11$

Step 3: Describe the pattern.

When finding the sum of 1 to 10, add the first and last numbers to get a result of 11. Then, add the second and second last numbers to get the same result. The pattern continues until all the numbers from 1 to 10 are added. There will be 5 pairs of such results. Since each addition equals 11, the answer is then $5 \times 11 = 55$.

Step 4: Use the pattern to find the answer.

Since there are 5 pairs in the sum of 1 to 10, there should be ($10 \times 5 = 50$ pairs) in the sum of 1 to 100.

Note that the addition for each pair is not equal to 11 now. The addition for each pair is now ($1 + 100 = 101$).

$$50 \times 101 = 5050$$

The sum of all the numbers from 1 to 100 is **5,050**.

5. Working Backward

The strategy of working backward applies only to a specific type of math word problem. These word problems state the end result, and students are required to find the total number. In order to solve these word problems, students have to work backward by thinking through the correct sequence of events. The strategy of working backward allows students to use their logical reasoning and sequencing to find the answers.

Example: Sarah has a piece of ribbon. She cuts the ribbon into 4 equal parts. Each part is then cut into 3 smaller equal parts. If the length of each small part is 35 cm, how long is the piece of ribbon?

$$3 \times 35 = 105 \text{ cm}$$
$$4 \times 105 = 420 \text{ cm}$$

The piece of ribbon is **420 cm**.

6. The Before-After Concept

The *Before-After* concept lists all the relevant data before and after an event. Students can then compare the differences and eventually solve the problems. Usually, the Before-After concept and the mathematical model go hand in hand to solve math word problems. Note that the Before-After concept can be applied only to a certain type of math word problem, which trains students to think sequentially.

Example: Kelly has 4 times as much money as Joey. After Kelly uses some money to buy a tennis racquet, and Joey uses $30 to buy a pair of pants, Kelly has twice as much money as Joey. If Joey has $98 in the beginning,
(a) how much money does Kelly have in the end?
(b) how much money does Kelly spend on the tennis racquet?

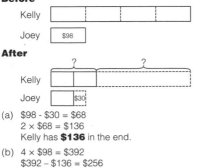

(a) $98 - $30 = $68
$2 \times $68 = 136
Kelly has **$136** in the end.

(b) $4 \times $98 = 392
$392 – $136 = 256
Kelly spends **$256** on the tennis racquet.

7. Making Supposition

Making supposition is commonly known as "making an assumption." Students can use this strategy to solve certain types of math word problems. Making

assumptions will eliminate some possibilities and simplifies the word problems by providing a boundary of values to work within.

Example: Mrs. Jackson bought 100 pieces of candy for all the students in her class. How many pieces of candy would each student receive if there were 25 students in her class?

In the above word problem, assume that each student received the same number of pieces. This eliminates the possibilities that some students would receive more than others due to good behaviour, better results, or any other reason.

8. Representation of Problem

In problem solving, students often use representations in the solutions to show their understanding of the problems. Using representations also allow students to understand the mathematical concepts and relationships as well as to manipulate the information presented in the problems. Examples of representations are diagrams and lists or tables.

Diagrams allow students to consolidate or organize the information given in the problems. By drawing a diagram, students can see the problem clearly and solve it effectively.

A list or table can help students organize information that is useful for analysis. After analyzing, students can then see a pattern, which can be used to solve the problem.

9. Guess and Check

One of the most important and effective problem-solving techniques is *Guess and Check*. It is also known as *Trial and Error*. As the name suggests, students have to guess the answer to a problem and check if that guess is correct. If the guess is wrong, students will make another guess. This will continue until the guess is correct.

It is beneficial to keep a record of all the guesses and checks in a table. In addition, a *Comments* column can be included. This will enable students to analyze their guess (if it is too high or too low) and improve on the next guess. Be careful; this problem-solving technique can be tiresome without systematic or logical guesses.

Example: Jessica had 15 coins. Some of them were 10-cent coins and the rest were 5-cent coins. The total amount added up to $1.25. How many coins of each kind were there?

Use the guess-and-check method.

Number of 10¢ Coins	Value	Number of 5¢ Coins	Value	Total Number of Coins	Total Value
7	$7 \times 10¢ = 70¢$	8	$8 \times 5¢ = 40¢$	$7 + 8 = 15$	$70¢ + 40¢ = 110¢$ $= 1.10
8	$8 \times 10¢ = 80¢$	7	$7 \times 5¢ = 35¢$	$8 + 7 = 15$	$80¢ + 35¢ = 115¢$ $= 1.15
10	$10 \times 10¢ = 100¢$	5	$5 \times 5¢ = 25¢$	$10 + 5 = 15$	$100¢ + 25¢ = 125¢$ $= 1.25

There were **ten** 10-cent coins and **five** 5-cent coins.

10. Restate the Problem

When solving challenging math problems, conventional methods may not be workable. Instead, restating the problem will enable students to see some challenging problems in a different light so that they can better understand them.

The strategy of restating the problem is to "say" the problem in a different and clearer way. However, students have to ensure that the main idea of the problem is not altered.

How do students restate a math problem?

First, read and understand the problem. Gather the given facts and unknowns. Note any condition(s) that have to be satisfied.

Next, restate the problem. Imagine narrating this problem to a friend. Present the given facts, unknown(s), and condition(s). Students may want to write the "revised" problem. Once the "revised" problem is analyzed, students should be able to think of an appropriate strategy to solve it.

11. Simplify the Problem

One of the commonly used strategies in mathematical problem solving is simplification of the problem. When a problem is simplified, it can be "broken down" into two or more smaller parts. Students can then solve the parts systematically to get to the final answer.

Table of Contents

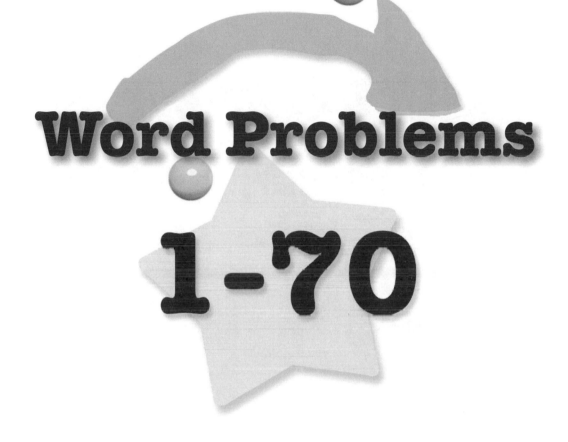

Word Problems 1-70

Question 1

Alex spent $\frac{3}{7}$ of his money. He gave $\frac{1}{4}$ of the remainder to his sister. He had $120 left. How much money did he have in the beginning?

Answer: _____

Question 2

Julio is 36 years old, and James is 11 years old. In how many years will Julio's age be twice James's age?

Answer: _____

Question 3

Lauren saved $84 more than Fiona. $\frac{1}{5}$ of Lauren's savings was the same as $\frac{3}{8}$ of Fiona's savings. How much did Lauren and Fiona save altogether?

Answer: _____

Question 4

A sum of money was divided among Jess, Adrian, and Mary in the ratio 4 : 3 : 5 respectively. Mary received $175.

(a) How much more money did Jess receive than Adrian?

(b) What was the sum of money?

Answer: (a) _____

(b) _____

Question 5

840 stickers were given to 42 children. $\frac{2}{3}$ of the children were boys, and each of them received the same number of stickers. Each girl received twice as many stickers as each boy. How many stickers did each girl receive?

Answer: _____

Mrs. Suarez bought 3 pairs of jeans and 5 shirts for $441. If each pair of jeans cost $\frac{2}{3}$ as much as each shirt,

(a)   what was the price of each pair of jeans?

(b)   what was the price of each shirt?

Answer: (a) _____

(b) _____

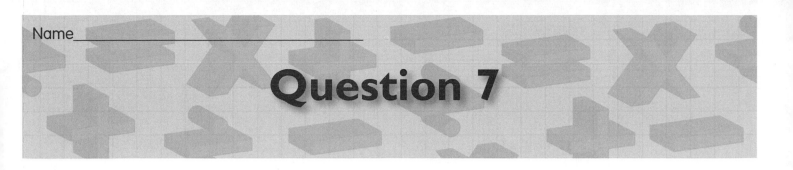

Question 7

Eric collected $1\frac{1}{3}$ times as many beads as Malik in the beginning. If Eric collected 48 more beads and Malik collected 13 more beads, Eric would have twice as many beads as Malik. How many beads did they collect altogether in the beginning?

Answer: _____

Mr. Cohen's monthly salary was $2,300 in December. His monthly salary increased by 15% in January. What was his salary in January?

Answer: _____

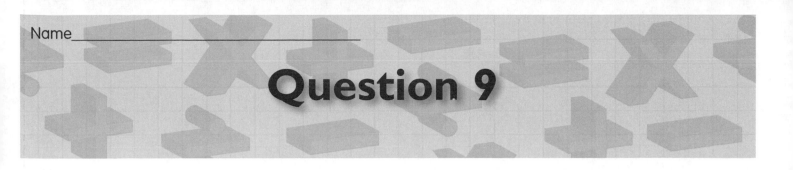

Question 9

Lea had $134, and Drew had $180. After both of them spent an equal amount of money shopping, Drew had 3 times as much money as Lea. How much did each of them spend?

Answer: _____

Question 10

A salesperson earns $80 for every computer he sells. He earns an additional $250 for every 10 computers he sells that month. How many computers does he need to sell in order to earn $2,340 in a month?

Answer: _____

Question 11

Mr. Williams paid $1,250 in cash for a new television set. If he had bought it using the store's payment plan, he would have had to pay a deposit of $350 and 9 monthly installments of $150. How much money did he save by paying in cash?

Answer: _____

Question 12

Mrs. Gorski bought a table and 6 chairs for $980. The table cost $524. Find the cost of 2 tables and 8 chairs.

Answer: _____

Question 13

A shopkeeper had 410 tangerines. He put some of them into 15 cartons containing 12 tangerines each. He then put the rest into 14 cartons, each containing the same number of tangerines.

(a)   How many tangerines were in each of the 14 cartons?

(b)   How many tangerines were left?

Answer: (a) _____

(b) _____

Question 14

Two cups, two plates, and a pot cost $10.20 at a yard sale. A cup costs twice as much as a plate. The pot costs $3 more than a cup. Find the cost of the pot.

Answer: _____

Question 15

A cabinet, 4 chairs, and 2 tables cost $825. The cabinet costs 3 times as much as a chair. The table costs $120 more than a chair. What is the cost of the cabinet?

Answer: _____

Question 16

Mrs. Sanders had 80 coins. Some of them were 1-dollar coins, and the rest were 50-cent coins. The total amount added up to $50. How many coins of each kind were there?

Answer: _____

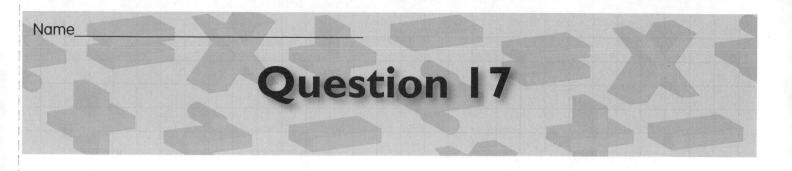

Question 17

Aaron and Henry had 52 grapes. If Aaron ate 11 grapes and gave 5 grapes to Henry, he would have 19 fewer grapes than Henry. How many grapes did Henry have in the beginning?

Answer: _____

Question 18

In a shop, there are 25 bicycles and tricycles. There are 63 wheels in all. Find the number of bicycles and tricycles in the shop.

Answer: _____

Question 19

A manager bought some stamps. She gave $\frac{1}{3}$ of them to a cashier and $\frac{1}{5}$ of them to her secretary. If the secretary received 40 fewer stamps than the cashier, how many stamps did the cashier receive?

Answer: _____

Question 20

Zoe, Minh, and Jake sold some tickets for a school fundraiser. Each ticket cost $2. Zoe sold $\frac{1}{2}$ of the tickets. Minh and Jake sold the remaining tickets in the ratio 1 : 3. If Zoe sold 36 more tickets than Minh, how much money did the 3 students collect altogether?

Answer: _____

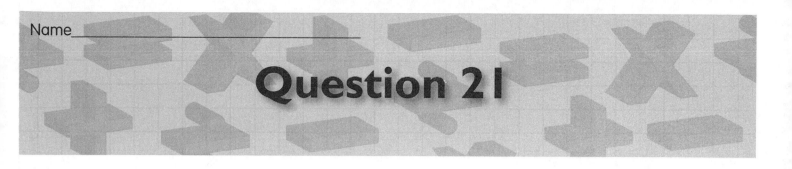

The ratio of the number of muffins Baker A baked to the number of muffins Baker B baked was 8 : 5. The ratio of the number of muffins Baker B baked to the number of muffins Baker C baked was 4 : 3. If Baker C baked 150 muffins, how many more muffins did Baker A bake than Baker C?

Answer: _____

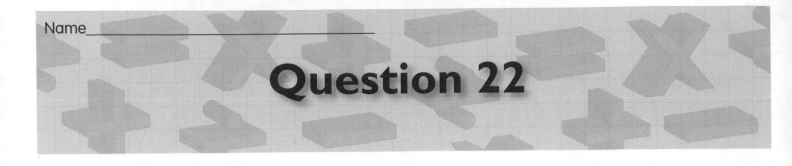

Question 22

There were 20 more apples in Basket A than in Basket B. Mr. Bell transferred 50 apples from Basket B to Basket A. There were 3 times as many apples in Basket A as in Basket B. How many apples were there altogether?

Answer: _____

Eduardo had 16 more stamps than Carson. $\frac{1}{2}$ of Carson's stamps were equal to $\frac{1}{4}$ of Eduardo's stamps.

(a)   How many stamps did Eduardo have?

(b)   After Eduardo gave away some stamps, he had $\frac{3}{8}$ as many stamps as Carson. How many stamps did Eduardo give away?

Answer: (a) _____

(b) _____

Mrs. Wen bought 500 markers for her students. She gave 8 markers to each girl and 10 markers to each boy. After giving the markers to all the boys and 12 girls, she had 54 markers left. How many more boys than girls were there?

Answer: _____

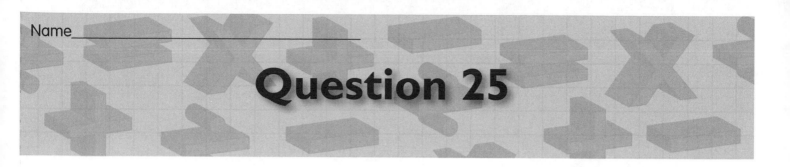

Question 25

After reading $\frac{3}{4}$ of a magazine on Sunday, 0.2 of the remainder on Monday, and 10 pages on Tuesday, Michael still had to read 42 pages of the magazine. How many pages did he read on Sunday?

Answer: _____

Question 26

The ratio of the number of Aaliyah's pens to the number of Mariah's pens was 2 : 3 at first. After Dad gave Aaliyah another 16 pens, the ratio became 2 : 1.

(a)   How many pens did Mariah have?

(b)   If Mariah gave away 6 pens, what would be the new ratio of the number of Aaliyah's pens (after Dad gave her 16 pens) to the number of Mariah's pens?

Answer: (a) _____

(b) _____

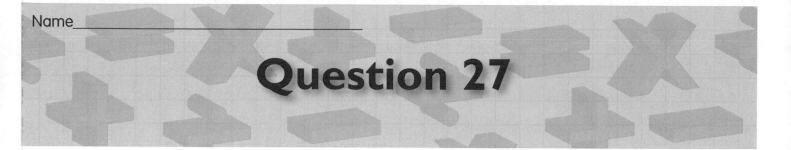

Question 27

The ratio of the number of Noah's stickers to the number of Jackson's stickers was 12 : 7. After Noah bought another 28 stickers and Jackson gave away 32 stickers, $\frac{5}{7}$ of Jackson's stickers were left.

(a)   How many more stickers did Noah have than Jackson in the beginning?

(b)   Find the new ratio of the number of Noah's stickers to the number of Jackson's stickers.

Answer: (a) _____

(b) _____

Question 28

The ratio of the number of Alex's beads to the number of Ellie's beads was 3 : 4. After Alex bought another 72 beads, the ratio became 3 : 1.

(a)   How many beads did Ellie have?

(b)   If Alex gave away 80 beads, what would be the new ratio of the number of Ellie's beads to the number of Alex's beads?

Answer: (a) _____

   (b) _____

Question 29

The ratio of Kwame's age to Derrick's age is 3 : 4. 2 years ago, their average age was 12 years. How old is Kwame now?

Answer: _____

Question 30

The ratio of Liam's age to his brother's age is 4 : 9. Liam is 10 years younger than his brother. How old is Liam now?

Answer: _____

Question 31

Joel had 219 marbles in 3 containers—A, B, and C. If he moved 21 marbles from Container A to Container B, 27 marbles from Container B to Container C, and 18 marbles from Container C to Container A, there would be an equal number of marbles in each container. How many marbles were in each container in the beginning?

Answer: _____

Bella spent $\frac{4}{7}$ of her money on a dictionary and 3 identical books. She spent $\frac{1}{6}$ of the remainder on a journal that cost $7.

(a)   How much did she spend on the dictionary and 3 books?

(b)   If $\frac{3}{8}$ of the cost of the dictionary was the same as $\frac{1}{2}$ of the total cost of 3 books, how much did each book cost?

Answer: (a) _____

(b) _____

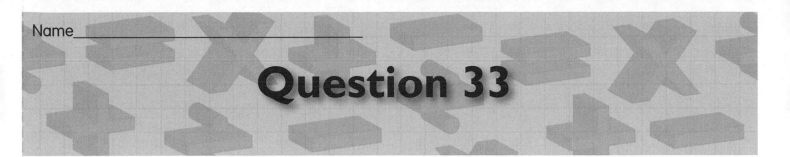

Question 33

Riley, Benny, and Claudia share a bag of peas in the ratio 4 : 3 : 8. If Claudia gives $\frac{1}{4}$ of her share to Benny, Benny will have 14 more peas than Riley. How many peas are there altogether?

Answer: _____

The mass of a jar is 750 g when it is $\frac{1}{2}$ filled with orange juice. The same jar has a mass of 625 g when it is $\frac{1}{4}$ filled with orange juice.

(a)   What is the mass of the jar when it is $\frac{3}{4}$ filled with orange juice?

(b)   What is the mass of the jar when it is empty?

Answer: (a) _____

(b) _____

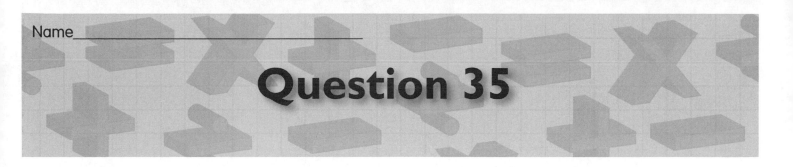

Question 35

Nadia has 3 times as many stamps as Evan and 50 more stamps than Kate. They have 972 stamps altogether. How many more stamps does Kate have than Evan?

Answer: _____

There are 24 girls and 18 boys in a class. What is the ratio of the number of boys to the total number of students in the class?

Answer: _____

Question 37

Jayden, Maggy, and Ramon shared $49 in the ratio 2 : 5 : 7. How much more did Ramon get than Jayden?

Answer: _____

There are 16 red buttons and some black buttons in a box. The ratio of the number of red buttons to that of black buttons is 2 : 3. If 5 red buttons are added into the box, what is the new ratio?

Answer: _____

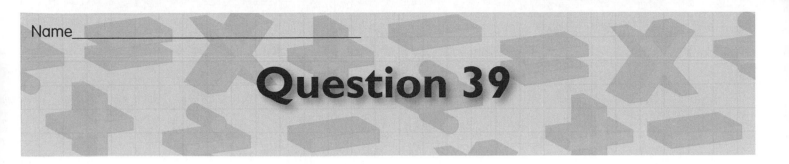

Question 39

The ratio of points scored by 3 boys on a math test is 7 : 10 : 12. If the sum of their scores is 232, what is the highest score?

Answer: _____

Question 40

Lucas had $272, and Kelly had $804. Both of them spent the same amount of money. The ratio of Lucas's money to Kelly's money then became 2 : 9. How much money did they spend altogether?

Answer: _____

Question 41

The ratio of the number of chickens to the number of ducks on a farm was 3 : 8. There were 40 more ducks than chickens. When half the chickens and some of the ducks were sold, the ratio of the number of chickens to the number of ducks became 3 : 4. How many ducks were sold?

Answer: _____

Cameron and Peter shared a box of markers in the ratio 5 : 3. Cameron gave half of his share to Peter. Peter then had 30 more markers than Cameron. How many markers did Cameron give to Peter?

Answer: _____

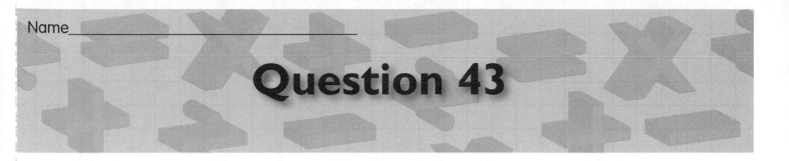

Question 43

Tierra and Joey shared some stamps in the ratio 7 : 5. Tierra gave Joey 12 stamps. If each of them had the same number of stamps in the end, how many stamps did Tierra have in the beginning?

Answer: _____

The ratio of Victoria's weight to Kazuki's weight was 4 : 5. If Victoria's weight increased by 5 lb. and Kazuki's weight decreased by 1 lb., Victoria would have the same weight as Kazuki. What was Victoria's original weight?

Answer: _____

Question 45

Last year, the ratio of the number of boys to the number of girls in the computer club was 1 : 2. This year, 70 new members joined the computer club. There are now 4 times as many boys and 3 times as many girls as last year. How many members were in the computer club last year?

Answer: _____

There were 85 erasers in Box A and 15 erasers in Box B. When an equal number of erasers was added to each box, the number of erasers in Box A was 3 times as many as that in Box B. How many erasers were added to each box?

Answer: _____

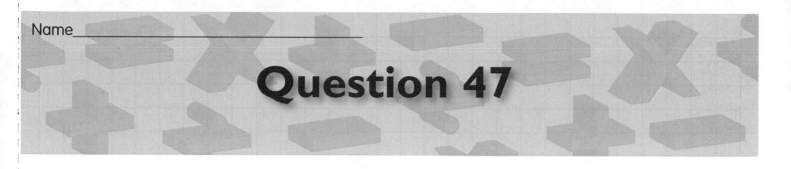

Question 47

A square plot of land has an area of 196 m², while a rectangular plot of land with a length of 12 m has an area of 96 m². What is the ratio of the length of the square plot of land to the width of the rectangular plot of land?

Answer: _____

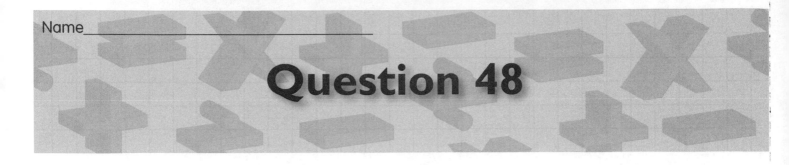

Question 48

Andrew had $93. With this money, he could buy 3 CDs and 4 books. However, he bought only 2 CDs and 3 books and had $27 left. What was the cost of each CD?

Answer: _____

The ratio of Carlos's money to Ava's money to Zach's money is 4 : 5 : 9. If Zach has $168 more than Ava,

(a)   how much money does Ava have?

(b)   how much money will Zach have left if he spends $\frac{1}{3}$ of it?

Answer: (a) _____

(b) _____

For every watch that Sarah sells, she earns $4. She gets an additional bonus of $50 for every 25 watches she sells. Last month, Sarah received a total of $506. How many watches did she sell last month?

Answer: _____

Question 51

Jamila and Akiko had the same amount of money to spend. After Jamila spent $33 and Akiko spent $42, Jamila had 4 times as much money left as Akiko. How much money did each of them have in the beginning?

Answer: _____

Question 52

Lily and Mackenzie collected some stamps. If Lily gave 4 stamps to Mackenzie, Mackenzie would have twice as many stamps as Lily. If Mackenzie gave 4 stamps to Lily, they would have the same number of stamps. How many stamps did each girl have?

Answer: _____

5 people can sit on each side of a square table. If 4 tables are pulled together to form a large square table, how many people can sit around the large table?

Answer: _____

Question 54

Josh had 240 seashells, and Brianna had 260 seashells. How many shells did Brianna give to Josh so that he would have 50 more shells than her?

Answer: _____

Question 55

Isaac and Paul shared some baseball cards in the ratio 2 : 5. If Paul gave 30 cards to Isaac, they would have the same number of cards. How many cards did Isaac have in the beginning?

Answer: _____

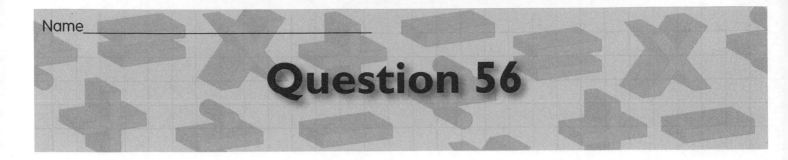

Question 56

The ratio of Beatriz's savings to Hannah's savings is 4 : 7. The ratio of Hannah's savings to Julia's savings is 3 : 5. The three girls have a total savings of $136. How much more money has Julia saved than Beatriz?

Answer: _____

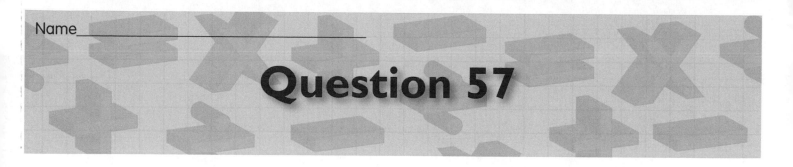

Question 57

Abby and Hakeem had the same number of CDs. After Abby gave away 28 CDs and Hakeem sold 17 CDs, the ratio of the number of Abby's CDs to the number of Hakeem's CDs became 2 : 3. How many CDs did they have altogether in the beginning?

Answer: _____

Question 58

The ratio of the number of cars to the number of SUVs in a parking lot is 3 : 1. The ratio of the number of SUVs to the number of minivans is 3 : 5.

(a) Find the ratio of the number of cars to the number of SUVs to the number of minivans in the parking lot.

(b) If there are 20 minivans, how many vehicles are there altogether?

Answer: (a) _____

(b) _____

Question 59

Sam, Jimmy, and Andre shared a number of pennies in the ratio 8 : 5 : 3. Sam and Andre received a total of 671 pennies. How many more pennies did Jimmy receive than Andre?

Answer: _____

Ally and Tony had a total of $44. After Ally spent $\frac{1}{4}$ of her money and Tony spent $5, the ratio of Ally's money to Tony's money became 1 : 2. How much money did Tony have in the beginning?

Answer: _____

Anne, Bridget, and Sasha shared a sum of money. Anne took $\frac{1}{3}$ of the total amount, and Bridget took $\frac{1}{4}$ of the remaining money. After both of them had taken their share, Sasha took $\frac{1}{2}$ of what was left. If Anne took $160, how much did Sasha take?

Answer: _____

Question 62

The ratio of the number of boys to the number of girls at an elementary school is 3 : 2. If each boy receives 2 pieces of paper and each girl receives 3 pieces, a total of 1,992 pieces of paper are needed. How many children are there altogether?

Answer: _____

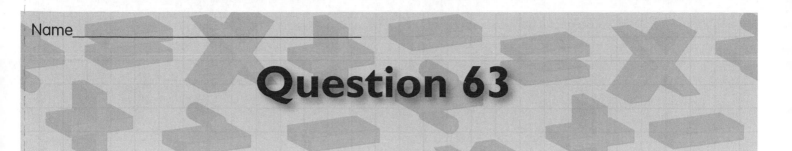
Jessica had 3 times as many postcards as Antonio. After Jessica gave 30 postcards to her friend and Antonio received 15 more postcards from his friend, Antonio had $\frac{3}{4}$ as many postcards as Jessica. How many postcards did they have altogether in the beginning?

Answer: _____

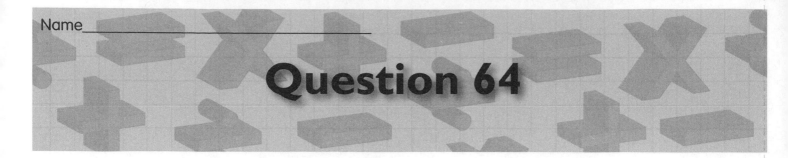

Question 64

Danny, Amira, and Tyler shared a sum of money in the ratio 6 : 4 : 3. Amira used $\frac{1}{2}$ of her money to buy a watch that cost $30, and Danny gave $\frac{1}{3}$ of his money to his sister. How much money did they have left altogether?

Answer: _____

Question 65

2 pencils and 3 pens cost $18.80. 6 pencils and 6 pens cost $45.

(a) How much is each pen?

(b) How much more does a pen cost than a pencil?

Answer: (a) _____

(b) _____

Question 66

Vincent paid $8.50 for 3 folders and a magazine. The magazine cost twice as much as a folder. What was the price of the magazine?

Answer: _____

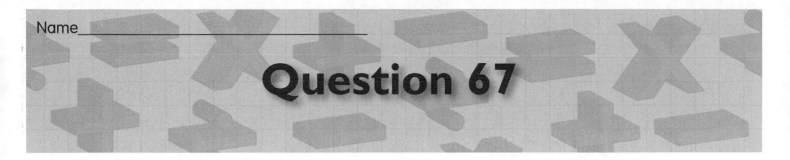

There is an equal number of 2 brands of watches on a shelf. Brand A watches cost $58 each, and Brand B watches cost $30 each. If the total cost of all the watches on the shelf is $22,000, how many watches are there?

Answer: _____

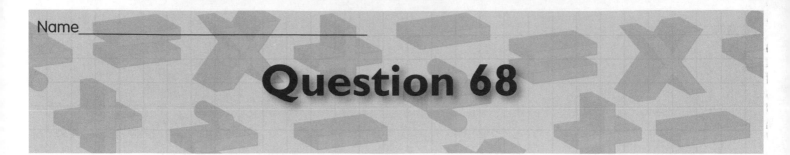
There were 28,000 people at a soccer match. $\frac{9}{14}$ of the people were men, $\frac{1}{7}$ were women, and the rest were children. If $\frac{3}{4}$ of the children were boys, how many girls were there?

Answer: _____

Question 69

Samantha, Cleo, and Elena had $780 altogether. Samantha had $40 more than Cleo, and Cleo had twice as much money as Elena. How much money did Cleo have?

Answer: _____

Taylor collected 3 times as many pebbles as Marco. Gina collected 21 fewer pebbles than Taylor. They collected 427 pebbles altogether. How many pebbles did Gina collect?

Answer: _____

Solutions to Word Problems 1-70

Solution to Question 1

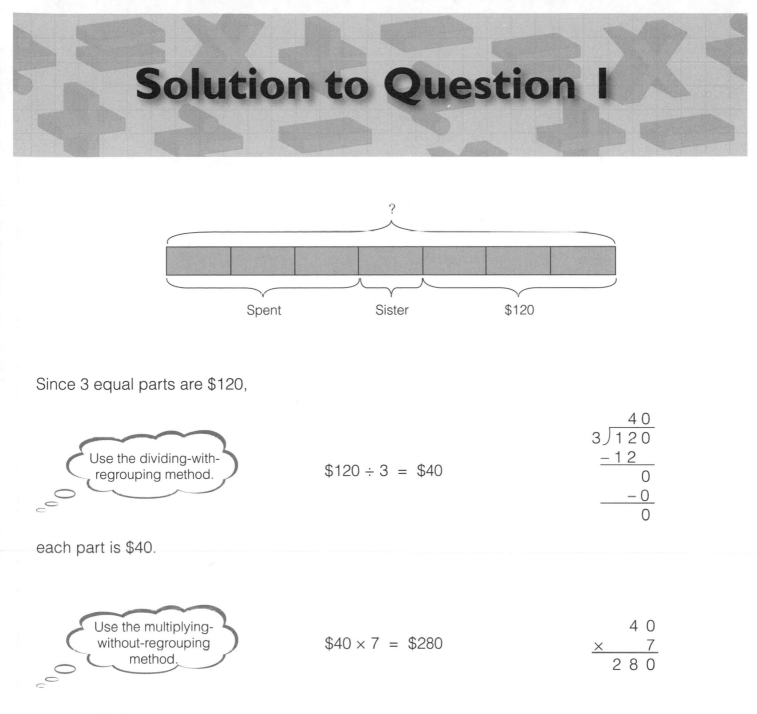

Since 3 equal parts are $120,

Use the dividing-with-regrouping method.

$120 ÷ 3 = $40

```
     4 0
  3 ) 1 2 0
    − 1 2
        0
      − 0
        0
```

each part is $40.

Use the multiplying-without-regrouping method.

$40 × 7 = $280

```
      4 0
  ×     7
    2 8 0
```

He had **$280** in the beginning.

Answer: **$280**

Solution to Question 2

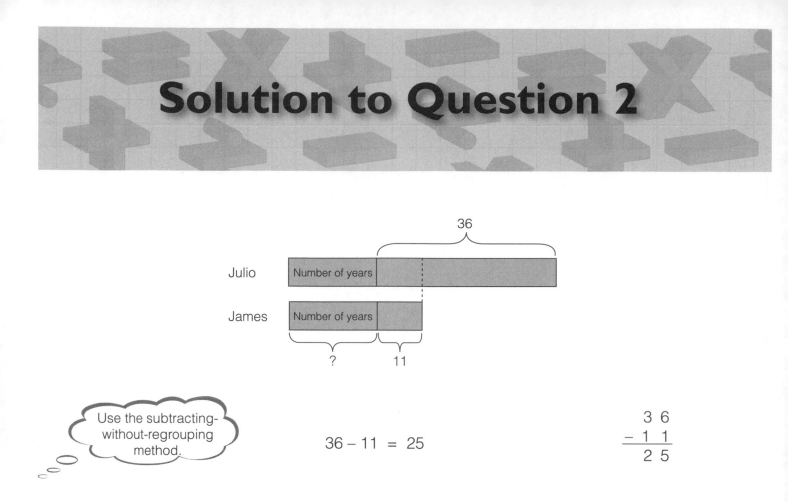

Use the subtracting-without-regrouping method.

$$36 - 11 = 25$$

$$\begin{array}{r} 3\ 6 \\ -\ 1\ 1 \\ \hline 2\ 5 \end{array}$$

James will be 25 years old when Julio is twice his age.

$$25 - 11 = 14$$

$$\begin{array}{r} 2\ 5 \\ -\ 1\ 1 \\ \hline 1\ 4 \end{array}$$

Julio's age will be twice James's age in **14** years.

Answer: __**14 years**__

Convert $\frac{1}{5}$ into its equivalent fraction in order to make the numerator common with $\frac{3}{8}$.

$$\frac{1\times3}{5\times3} = \frac{3}{15}$$

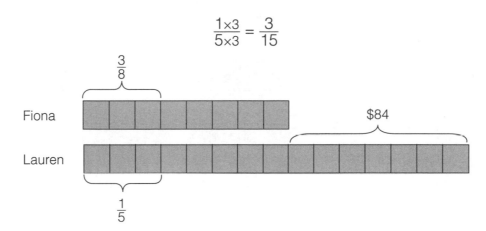

Since 7 equal parts are $84,

Use the dividing-with-regrouping method.

$84 ÷ 7 = $12

$$\begin{array}{r} 1\,2 \\ 7\overline{)8\,4} \\ -7 \\ \hline 1\,4 \\ -1\,4 \\ \hline 0 \end{array}$$

each part is $12.

Use the multiplying-without-regrouping method.

$12 × 23 = $276

$$\begin{array}{r} 2\,3 \\ \times\ 1\,2 \\ \hline 4\,6 \\ +\ 2\,3 \\ \hline 2\,7\,6 \end{array}$$

Lauren and Fiona saved **$276** altogether.

Answer: **$276**

Solution to Question 4

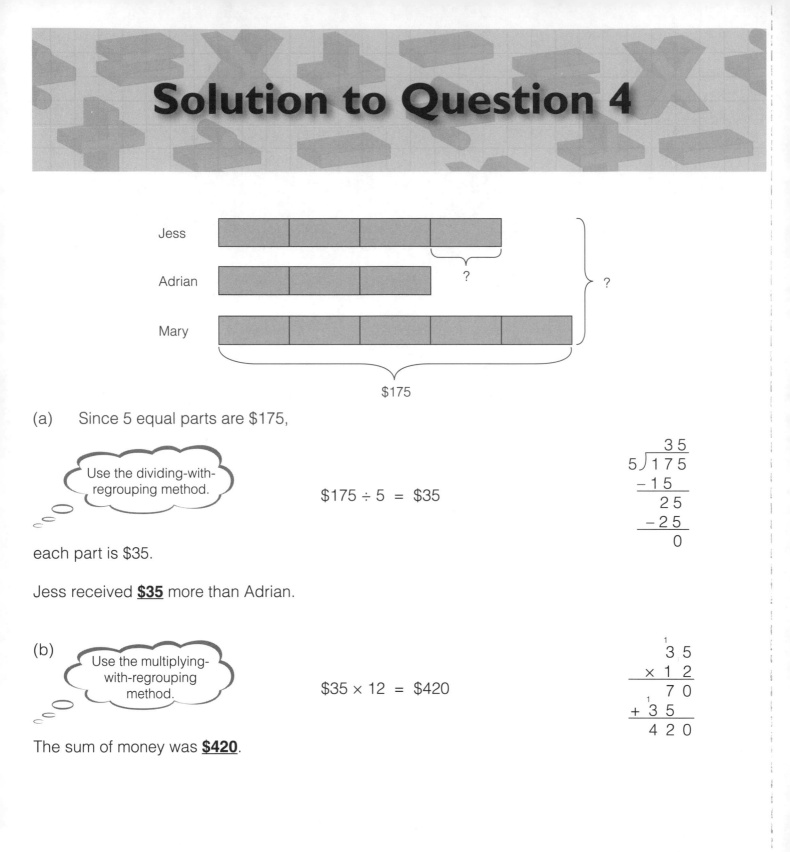

Jess

Adrian ?

Mary ?

$175

(a)   Since 5 equal parts are $175,

> Use the dividing-with-regrouping method.

$175 \div 5 = \$35$

```
      3 5
  5 ) 1 7 5
    - 1 5
      2 5
    - 2 5
        0
```

each part is $35.

Jess received **$35** more than Adrian.

(b)
> Use the multiplying-with-regrouping method.

$\$35 \times 12 = \$420$

```
      ¹
      3 5
    × 1 2
      7 0
   ¹
  + 3 5
    4 2 0
```

The sum of money was **$420**.

Answer: (a) _____**$35**_____

(b) _____**$420**_____

Solution to Question 5

> Use the subtraction-of-fractions method.

$$1 - \frac{2}{3} = \frac{3}{3} - \frac{2}{3}$$
$$= \frac{1}{3}$$

$\frac{1}{3}$ of the children were girls.

> Use the multiplication-of-fractions method.

$$\frac{1}{3_1} \times \overset{14}{\cancel{42}} = 14$$

$$\begin{array}{r} 14 \\ 3\overline{)42} \\ -3 \\ \hline 12 \\ -12 \\ \hline 0 \end{array}$$

There were 14 girls. There were 28 boys.

Since each girl received twice as many stickers as each boy, the number of stickers shared by the boys and girls should be the same.

> Use the dividing-with-regrouping method.

$$840 \div 2 = 420$$

$$\begin{array}{r} 420 \\ 2\overline{)840} \\ -8 \\ \hline 4 \\ 4 \\ \hline 0 \\ -0 \\ \hline 0 \end{array}$$

The girls received 420 stickers in total.

$$420 \div 14 = 30$$

$$\begin{array}{r} 30 \\ 14\overline{)420} \\ -42 \\ \hline 0 \\ -0 \\ \hline 0 \end{array}$$

Each girl received **30** stickers.

Answer: **30 stickers**

Solution to Question 6

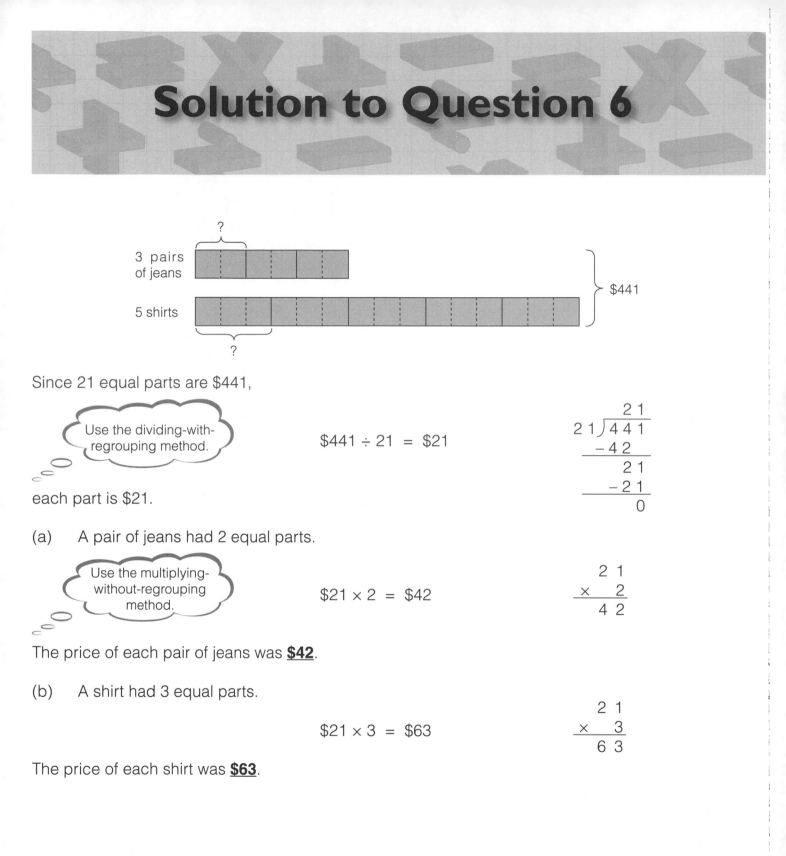

Since 21 equal parts are $441,

Use the dividing-with-regrouping method.

$$\$441 \div 21 = \$21$$

$$\begin{array}{r} 21 \\ 21\overline{)441} \\ -42 \\ \hline 21 \\ -21 \\ \hline 0 \end{array}$$

each part is $21.

(a)   A pair of jeans had 2 equal parts.

Use the multiplying-without-regrouping method.

$$\$21 \times 2 = \$42$$

$$\begin{array}{r} 21 \\ \times\ \ 2 \\ \hline 42 \end{array}$$

The price of each pair of jeans was **$42**.

(b)   A shirt had 3 equal parts.

$$\$21 \times 3 = \$63$$

$$\begin{array}{r} 21 \\ \times\ \ 3 \\ \hline 63 \end{array}$$

The price of each shirt was **$63**.

Answer: (a) _____**$42**_____

(b) _____**$63**_____

Convert $1\frac{1}{3}$ into an improper fraction, $1\frac{1}{3} = \frac{4}{3}$

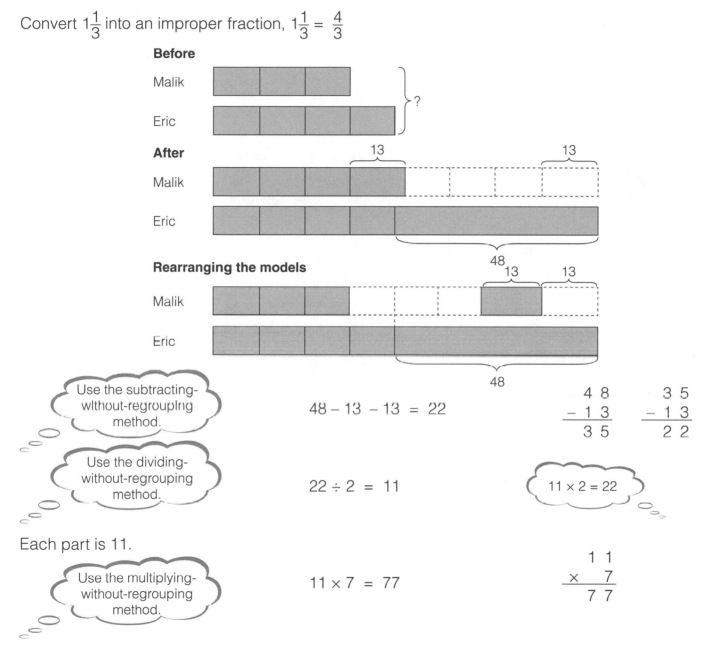

48 − 13 − 13 = 22

$$\begin{array}{r} 4\ 8 \\ -\ 1\ 3 \\ \hline 3\ 5 \end{array} \qquad \begin{array}{r} 3\ 5 \\ -\ 1\ 3 \\ \hline 2\ 2 \end{array}$$

22 ÷ 2 = 11

11 × 2 = 22

Each part is 11.

11 × 7 = 77

$$\begin{array}{r} 1\ 1 \\ \times\ \ \ 7 \\ \hline 7\ 7 \end{array}$$

They collected **77** beads altogether in the beginning.

Answer: _____**77 beads**_____

Change 15% to its fraction form.

$$15\% = \frac{15}{100}$$

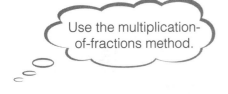

Use the multiplication-of-fractions method.

$$\frac{15}{1\cancel{0}\cancel{0}} \times \$2,3\cancel{0}\cancel{0} = \$345$$

$$
\begin{array}{r}
{}^{1}{}_{1} \\
1\ 5 \\
\times\ 2\ 3 \\
\hline
4\ 5 \\
+\ 3\ 0 \\
\hline
3\ 4\ 5
\end{array}
$$

Mr. Cohen's monthly salary increased by $345.

Use the adding-without-regrouping method.

$$\$2,300 + \$345 = \$2,645$$

$$
\begin{array}{r}
2,3\ 0\ 0 \\
+\ \ \ 3\ 4\ 5 \\
\hline
2,6\ 4\ 5
\end{array}
$$

His salary in January was **$2,645**.

Answer: _____**$2,645**_____

Solution to Question 9

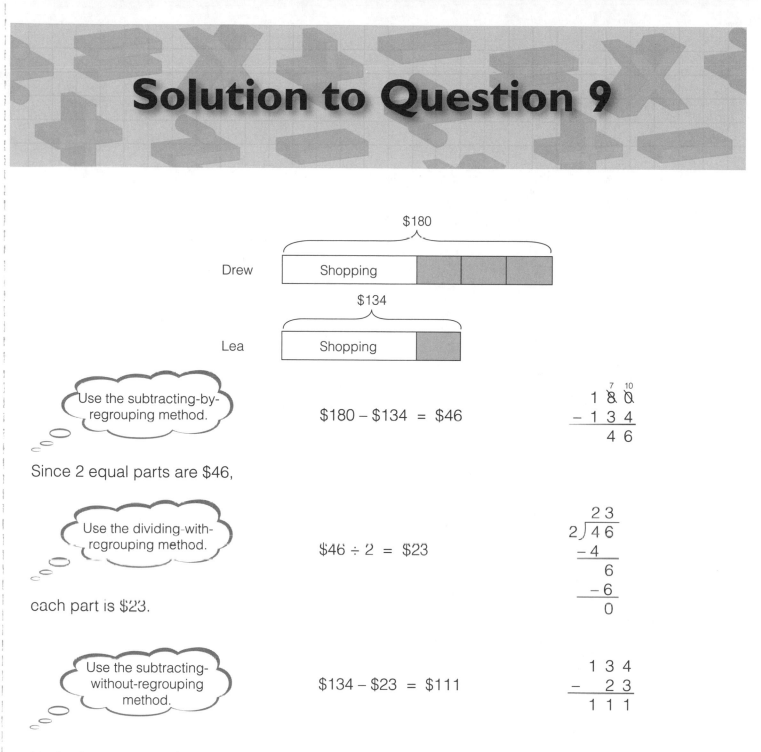

$180

Drew | Shopping

$134

Lea | Shopping

Use the subtracting-by-regrouping method.

$180 − $134 = $46

$$\begin{array}{r} 1\ \overset{7}{\cancel{8}}\ \overset{10}{\cancel{0}} \\ -\ 1\ 3\ 4 \\ \hline 4\ 6 \end{array}$$

Since 2 equal parts are $46,

Use the dividing-with-regrouping method.

$46 ÷ 2 = $23

$$\begin{array}{r} 23 \\ 2\overline{\smash{)}46} \\ -4 \\ \hline 6 \\ -6 \\ \hline 0 \end{array}$$

each part is $23.

Use the subtracting-without-regrouping method.

$134 − $23 = $111

$$\begin{array}{r} 1\ 3\ 4 \\ -\ \ \ 2\ 3 \\ \hline 1\ 1\ 1 \end{array}$$

Each of them spent **$111**.

Answer: _____**$111**_____

Solution to Question 10

$$?$$

| $80 | $80 | $80 | $80 | $80 | $80 | $80 | $80 | $80 | $80 | $250 |

Use the multiplying-without-regrouping method.

$$\$80 \times 10 = \$800$$

Use the adding-without-regrouping method.

$$\$800 + \$250 = \$1,050$$

$$
\begin{array}{r}
8\ 0\ 0 \\
+\ \ 2\ 5\ 0 \\
\hline
1,\ 0\ 5\ 0
\end{array}
$$

He could earn $1,050 if he sells 10 computers in a month.

Use the multiplying-with-regrouping method.

$$\$1,050 \times 2 = \$2,100$$

$$
\begin{array}{r}
\overset{1}{1,}\ 0\ 5\ 0 \\
\times\ \ \ \ \ \ \ \ \ 2 \\
\hline
2,\ 1\ 0\ 0
\end{array}
$$

He could earn $2,100 if he sells 20 computers in a month.

Use the subtracting-without-regrouping method.

$$\$2,340 - \$2,100 = \$240$$

$$
\begin{array}{r}
2,\ 3\ 4\ 0 \\
-\ 2,\ 1\ 0\ 0 \\
\hline
2\ 4\ 0
\end{array}
$$

Use the dividing-with-regrouping method.

$$\$240 \div \$80 = 3$$

$$
\begin{array}{r}
3\ \ \ \\
80\overline{)2\ 4\ 0} \\
-2\ 4\ 0 \\
\hline
0
\end{array}
$$

He must sell 3 computers to earn $240.

$$20 + 3 = 23$$

He needs to sell **23** computers in order to earn $2,340 in a month.

Answer: __23 computers__

Solution to Question 11

Use the multiplying-with-regrouping method.

$$\$150 \times 9 = \$1,350$$

$$\begin{array}{r} \overset{4}{1}\ 5\ 0 \\ \times \quad\ \ 9 \\ \hline 1,\ 3\ 5\ 0 \end{array}$$

Use the adding-by-regrouping method.

$$\$1,350 + \$350 = \$1,700$$

$$\begin{array}{r} 1,\ \overset{1}{3}\ 5\ 0 \\ +\quad 3\ 5\ 0 \\ \hline 1,\ 7\ 0\ 0 \end{array}$$

He would have had to pay $1,700 if he had bought it using the store's payment plan.

Use the subtracting-by-regrouping method.

$$\$1,700 - \$1,250 = \$450$$

$$\begin{array}{r} 1,\ \overset{6}{\cancel{7}}\ \overset{10}{\cancel{0}}\ 0 \\ -\ 1,\ 2\ 5\ 0 \\ \hline 4\ 5\ 0 \end{array}$$

He saved **$450** by paying in cash.

Answer: _____ **$450** _____

Solution to Question 12

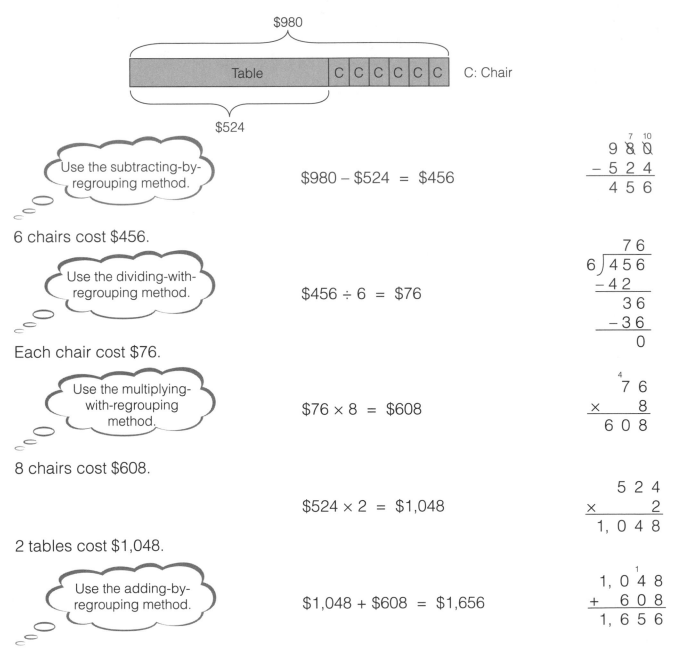

Use the subtracting-by-regrouping method.

$980 - $524 = $456

$$\begin{array}{r} 9\ \overset{7}{\cancel{8}}\ \overset{10}{\cancel{0}} \\ -\ 5\ 2\ 4 \\ \hline 4\ 5\ 6 \end{array}$$

6 chairs cost $456.

Use the dividing-with-regrouping method.

$456 ÷ 6 = $76

$$\begin{array}{r} 7\ 6 \\ 6\overline{)4\ 5\ 6} \\ -4\ 2 \\ \hline 3\ 6 \\ -3\ 6 \\ \hline 0 \end{array}$$

Each chair cost $76.

Use the multiplying-with-regrouping method.

$76 × 8 = $608

$$\begin{array}{r} \overset{4}{7}\ 6 \\ \times\ \ \ 8 \\ \hline 6\ 0\ 8 \end{array}$$

8 chairs cost $608.

$524 × 2 = $1,048

$$\begin{array}{r} 5\ 2\ 4 \\ \times\ \ \ \ 2 \\ \hline 1,\ 0\ 4\ 8 \end{array}$$

2 tables cost $1,048.

Use the adding-by-regrouping method.

$1,048 + $608 = $1,656

$$\begin{array}{r} 1,\ 0\ \overset{1}{4}\ 8 \\ +\ \ \ 6\ 0\ 8 \\ \hline 1,\ 6\ 5\ 6 \end{array}$$

The cost of 2 tables and 8 chairs was **$1,656**.

Answer: _____**$1,656**_____

Solution to Question 13

Use the multiplying-with-regrouping method.

$$15 \times 12 = 180$$

$$
\begin{array}{r}
{}^{1} \\
1\ 5 \\
\times\ 1\ 2 \\
\hline
3\ 0 \\
+\ 1\ 5 \\
\hline
1\ 8\ 0
\end{array}
$$

180 tangerines were packed into 15 cartons.

Use the subtracting-by-regrouping method.

$$410 - 180 = 230$$

$$
\begin{array}{r}
{}^{3}\ {}^{11} \\
\cancel{4}\ \cancel{1}\ 0 \\
-\ 1\ 8\ 0 \\
\hline
2\ 3\ 0
\end{array}
$$

230 tangerines were packed into 14 cartons.

(a) Use the dividing-with-regrouping method.

$$230 \div 14 = 16\ R\ 6$$

$$
\begin{array}{r}
16 \\
14\overline{)230} \\
-14 \\
\hline
90 \\
-84 \\
\hline
6
\end{array}
$$

There were **16** tangerines in each of the 14 cartons.

(b)   **6** tangerines were left.

Answer: (a) __**16 tangerines**__

(b) __**6 tangerines**__

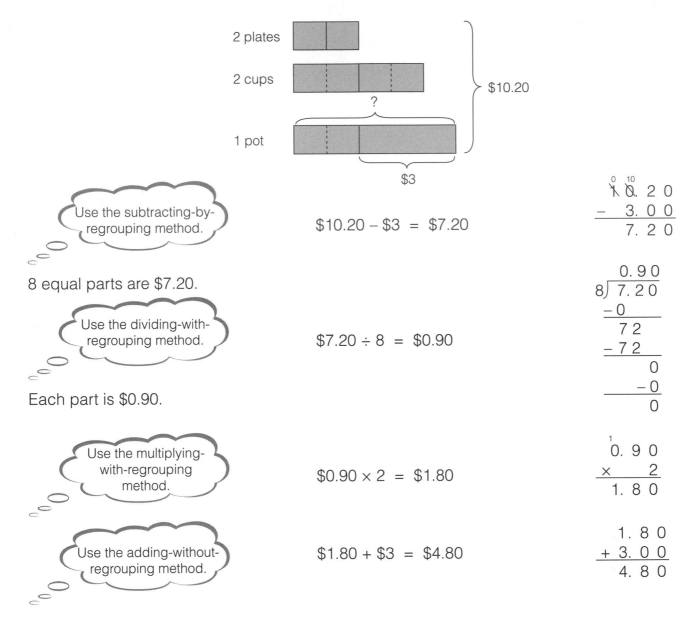

Use the subtracting-by-regrouping method.

$10.20 − $3 = $7.20

8 equal parts are $7.20.

Use the dividing-with-regrouping method.

$7.20 ÷ 8 = $0.90

Each part is $0.90.

Use the multiplying-with-regrouping method.

$0.90 × 2 = $1.80

Use the adding-without-regrouping method.

$1.80 + $3 = $4.80

The cost of the pot is **$4.80**.

Answer: _____ **$4.80**

Solution to Question 15

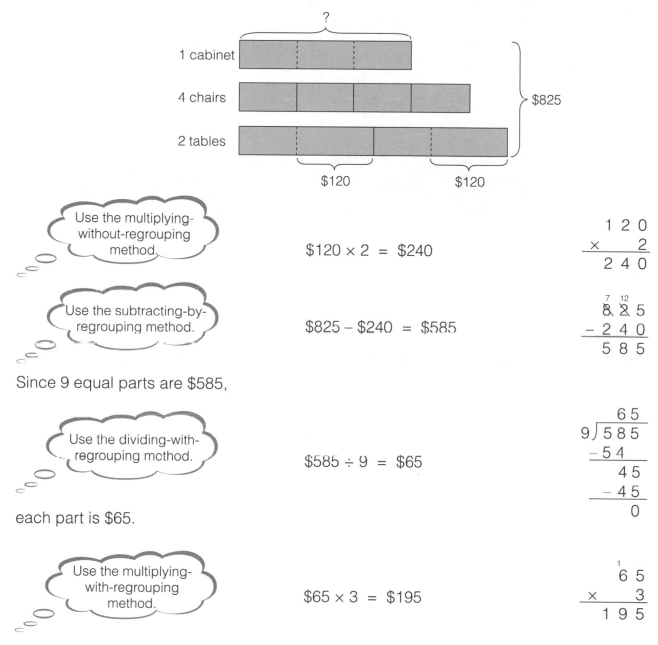

Use the multiplying-without-regrouping method.

$120 × 2 = $240

$$\begin{array}{r} 1\ 2\ 0 \\ \times\quad 2 \\ \hline 2\ 4\ 0 \end{array}$$

Use the subtracting-by-regrouping method.

$825 − $240 = $585

$$\begin{array}{r} 8\ 2\ 5 \\ -\ 2\ 4\ 0 \\ \hline 5\ 8\ 5 \end{array}$$

Since 9 equal parts are $585,

Use the dividing-with-regrouping method.

$585 ÷ 9 = $65

$$\begin{array}{r} 65 \\ 9\overline{)585} \\ -54 \\ \hline 45 \\ -45 \\ \hline 0 \end{array}$$

each part is $65.

Use the multiplying-with-regrouping method.

$65 × 3 = $195

$$\begin{array}{r} 6\ 5 \\ \times\quad 3 \\ \hline 1\ 9\ 5 \end{array}$$

The cost of the cabinet is **$195**.

Answer: _____**$195**_____

Use the guess-and-check method.

Use the multiplying-without-regrouping method.

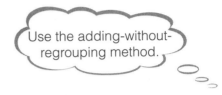

Use the adding-without-regrouping method.

Number of $1 coins	Value	Number of 50¢ coins	Value	Total number of coins	Total value
40	40 × $1 = $40	40	40 × 50¢ = 2,000¢ = $20	40 + 40 = 80	$40 + $20 = $60
30	30 × $1 = $30	50	50 × 50¢ = 2,500¢ = $25	30 + 50 = 80	$30 + $25 = $55
20	**20 × $1 = $20**	**60**	**60 × 50¢ = 3,000¢ = $30**	**20 + 60 = 80**	**$20 + $30 = $50**

There were **twenty** 1-dollar coins and **sixty** 50-cent coins.

Answer: **twenty 1-dollar coins; sixty 50-cent coins**

$$52 - 11 = 41$$

After eating 11 grapes, Aaron and Henry had 41 grapes.

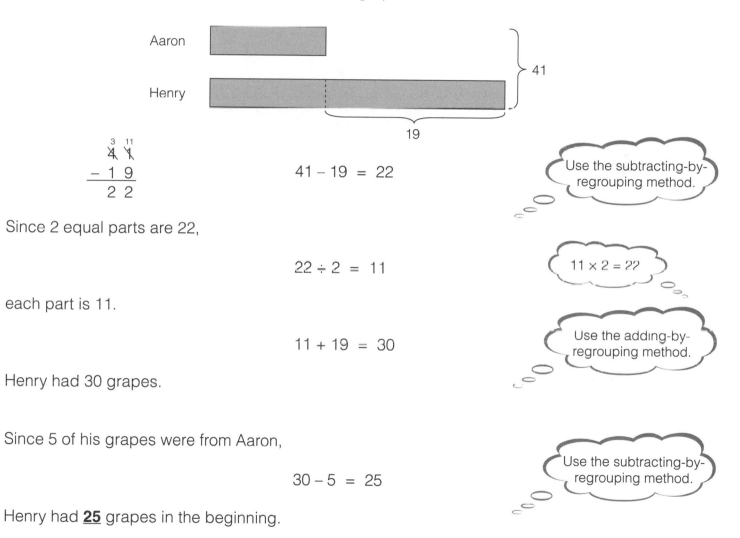

Aaron

Henry

41

19

$$
\begin{array}{r}
\overset{3}{\cancel{4}}\ \overset{11}{\cancel{1}} \\
-\ 1\ 9 \\
\hline
2\ 2
\end{array}
$$

$$41 - 19 = 22$$

Use the subtracting-by-regrouping method.

Since 2 equal parts are 22,

$$22 \div 2 = 11$$

$11 \times 2 = 22$

each part is 11.

$$11 + 19 = 30$$

Use the adding-by-regrouping method.

Henry had 30 grapes.

Since 5 of his grapes were from Aaron,

$$30 - 5 = 25$$

Use the subtracting-by-regrouping method.

Henry had **25** grapes in the beginning.

Answer: __**25 grapes**__

A bicycle has 2 wheels.

A tricycle has 3 wheels.

Use the adding-without-regrouping method.

$2 + 3 = 5$

One bicycle and one tricycle have 5 wheels altogether.

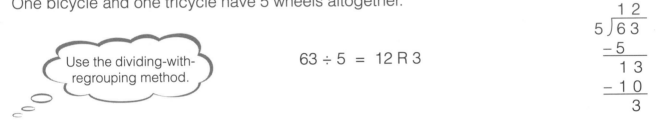

Use the dividing-with-regrouping method.

$63 \div 5 = 12 \text{ R } 3$

$$\begin{array}{r} 1\ 2 \\ 5\overline{)6\ 3} \\ -5 \\ \hline 1\ 3 \\ -1\ 0 \\ \hline 3 \end{array}$$

12 bicycles and 12 tricycles have 60 wheels.

The remaining 3 wheels must belong to a tricycle.

There are **12** bicycles and **13** tricycles.

Answer: **12 bicycles and 13 tricycles**

Convert $\frac{1}{3}$ and $\frac{1}{5}$ into equivalent fractions.

$$\frac{1 \times 5}{3 \times 5} = \frac{5}{15}$$

$$\frac{1 \times 3}{5 \times 3} = \frac{3}{15}$$

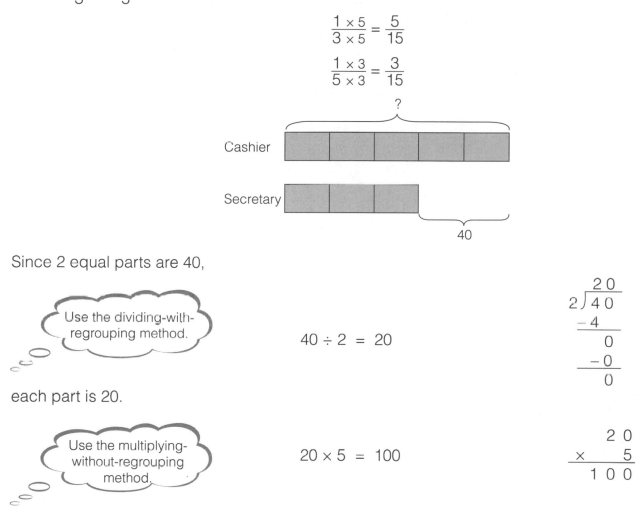

Since 2 equal parts are 40,

Use the dividing-with-regrouping method.

$$40 \div 2 = 20$$

$$\begin{array}{r} 20 \\ 2\overline{)40} \\ -4 \\ \hline 0 \\ -0 \\ \hline 0 \end{array}$$

each part is 20.

Use the multiplying-without-regrouping method.

$$20 \times 5 = 100$$

$$\begin{array}{r} 20 \\ \times 5 \\ \hline 100 \end{array}$$

The cashier received **100** stamps.

Answer: **100 stamps**

Solution to Question 20

Zoe

Minh | Jake | Jake | Jake

Since 3 equal parts are 36,

Use the dividing-with-regrouping method.

$36 \div 3 = 12$

```
  1 2
3 ) 3 6
  - 3
    6
  - 6
    0
```

each part is 12.

Use the multiplying-with-regrouping method.

$12 \times 8 = 96$

```
    ¹1 2
  ×   8
    9 6
```

The 3 students sold 96 tickets altogether.

Use the multiplying-with-regrouping method.

$96 \times \$2 = \$192$

```
    ¹9 6
  ×   2
  1 9 2
```

They collected **$192** altogether.

Answer: _____**$192**_____

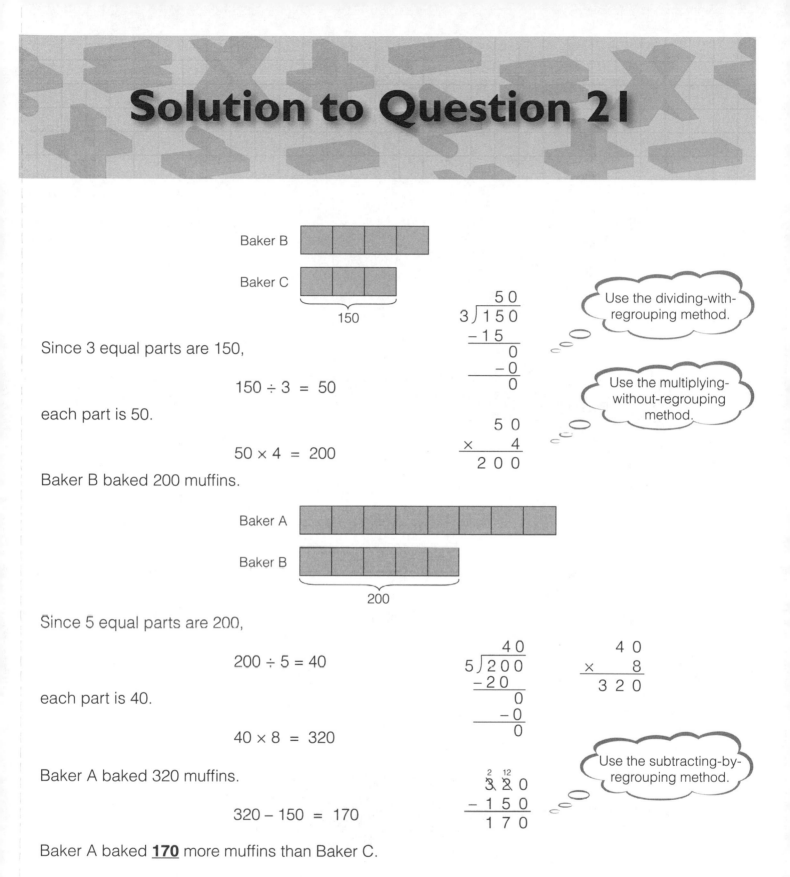

Baker B

Baker C

150

Since 3 equal parts are 150,

$$150 \div 3 = 50$$

each part is 50.

$$50 \times 4 = 200$$

Baker B baked 200 muffins.

$$
\begin{array}{r}
50 \\
3\overline{)150} \\
-15 \\
\hline
0 \\
-0 \\
\hline
0
\end{array}
$$

Use the dividing-with-regrouping method.

$$
\begin{array}{r}
50 \\
\times \quad 4 \\
\hline
200
\end{array}
$$

Use the multiplying-without-regrouping method.

Baker A

Baker B

200

Since 5 equal parts are 200,

$$200 \div 5 = 40$$

each part is 40.

$$40 \times 8 = 320$$

Baker A baked 320 muffins.

$$320 - 150 = 170$$

$$
\begin{array}{r}
40 \\
5\overline{)200} \\
-20 \\
\hline
0 \\
-0 \\
\hline
0
\end{array}
\qquad
\begin{array}{r}
40 \\
\times \quad 8 \\
\hline
320
\end{array}
$$

$$
\begin{array}{r}
{\scriptstyle 2\ 12} \\
3\!\!\!/\,2\!\!\!/\,0 \\
-150 \\
\hline
170
\end{array}
$$

Use the subtracting-by-regrouping method.

Baker A baked **170** more muffins than Baker C.

Answer: **170 more muffins**

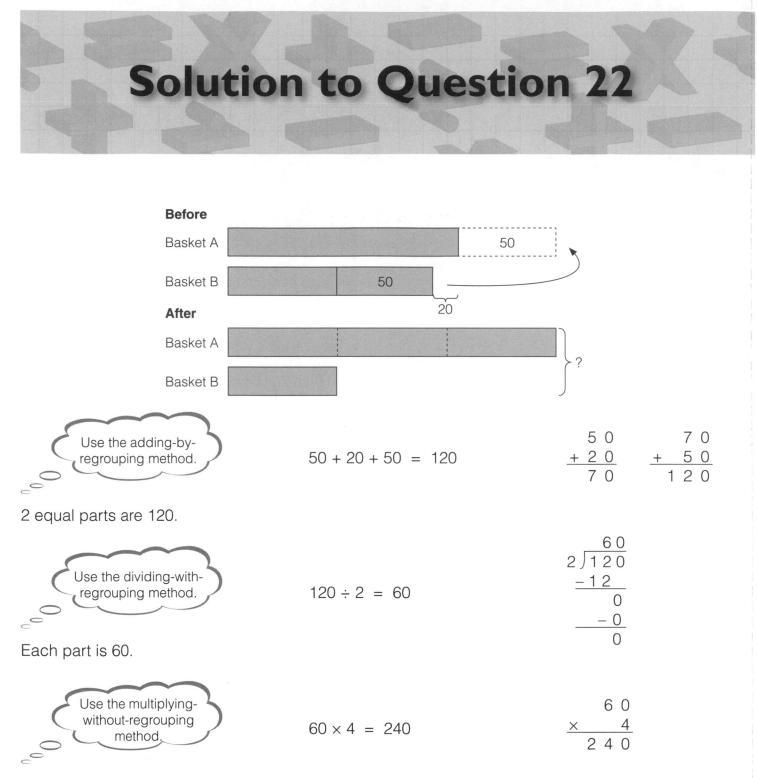

Before

Basket A

Basket B

50

20

After

Basket A

Basket B

?

Use the adding-by-regrouping method.

$50 + 20 + 50 = 120$

```
  5 0
+ 2 0
  7 0
```

```
  7 0
+ 5 0
1 2 0
```

2 equal parts are 120.

Use the dividing-with-regrouping method.

$120 \div 2 = 60$

```
      6 0
  2 ) 1 2 0
    - 1 2
        0
      - 0
        0
```

Each part is 60.

Use the multiplying-without-regrouping method.

$60 \times 4 = 240$

```
    6 0
×      4
  2 4 0
```

There were **240** apples altogether.

Answer: __**240 apples**__

Solution to Question 23

(a)

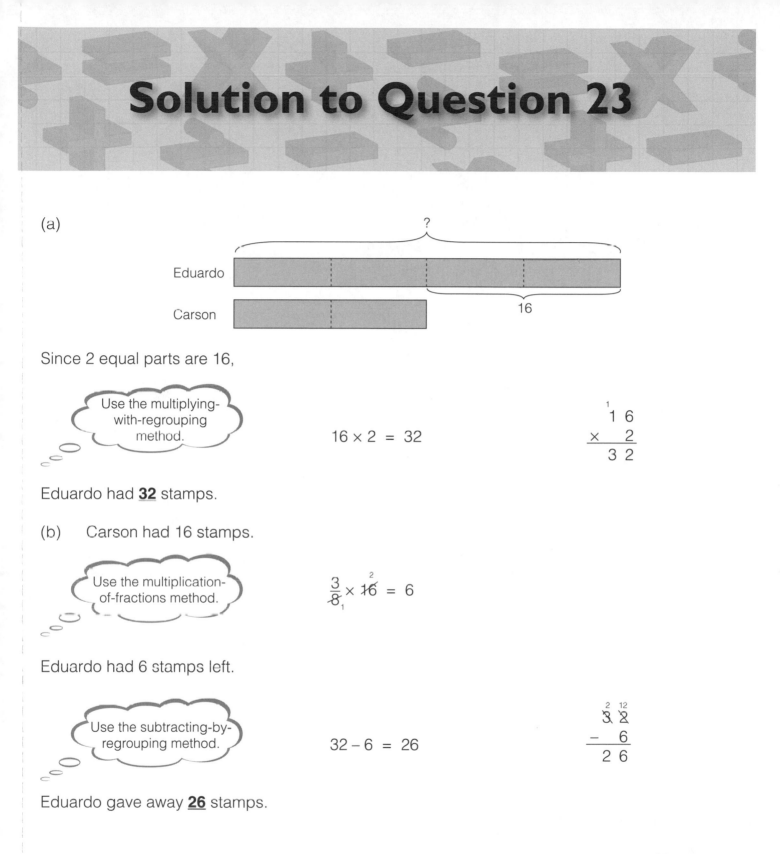

Eduardo

Carson

16

Since 2 equal parts are 16,

Use the multiplying-with-regrouping method.

$16 \times 2 = 32$

$$\begin{array}{r} {}^{1} \\ 1\,6 \\ \times 2 \\ \hline 3\,2 \end{array}$$

Eduardo had **32** stamps.

(b)   Carson had 16 stamps.

Use the multiplication-of-fractions method.

$\dfrac{3}{8} \times \overset{2}{16} = 6$

Eduardo had 6 stamps left.

Use the subtracting-by-regrouping method.

$32 - 6 = 26$

$$\begin{array}{r} {}^{2}{}^{12} \\ \cancel{3}\,\cancel{2} \\ -6 \\ \hline 2\,6 \end{array}$$

Eduardo gave away **26** stamps.

Answer: (a) __**32 stamps**__

(b) __**26 stamps**__

Solution to Question 24

Use the subtracting-with-regrouping method.

$500 - 54 = 446$

$$\begin{array}{r} {}^{4}\cancel{5}\,{}^{9}\cancel{0}\,{}^{10}\cancel{0} \\ -\quad 5\ 4 \\ \hline 4\ 4\ 6 \end{array}$$

Mrs. Wen gave away a total of 446 markers.

Use the multiplying-with-regrouping method.

$8 \times 12 = 96$

$$\begin{array}{r} {}^{1}\ \ \\ 1\ 2 \\ \times\quad 8 \\ \hline 9\ 6 \end{array}$$

She gave 96 markers to 12 girls.

$446 - 96 = 350$

$$\begin{array}{r} {}^{3}\cancel{4}\,{}^{14}\cancel{4}\ 6 \\ -\quad 9\ 6 \\ \hline 3\ 5\ 0 \end{array}$$

She gave 350 markers to the boys.

Use the dividing-without-regrouping method.

$350 \div 10 = 35$

There were 35 boys.

Use the subtracting-without-regrouping method.

$35 - 12 = 23$

$$\begin{array}{r} 3\ 5 \\ -\ 1\ 2 \\ \hline 2\ 3 \end{array}$$

There were **23** more boys than girls.

Answer: __**23 more boys**__

Convert the decimal 0.2 to a fraction.

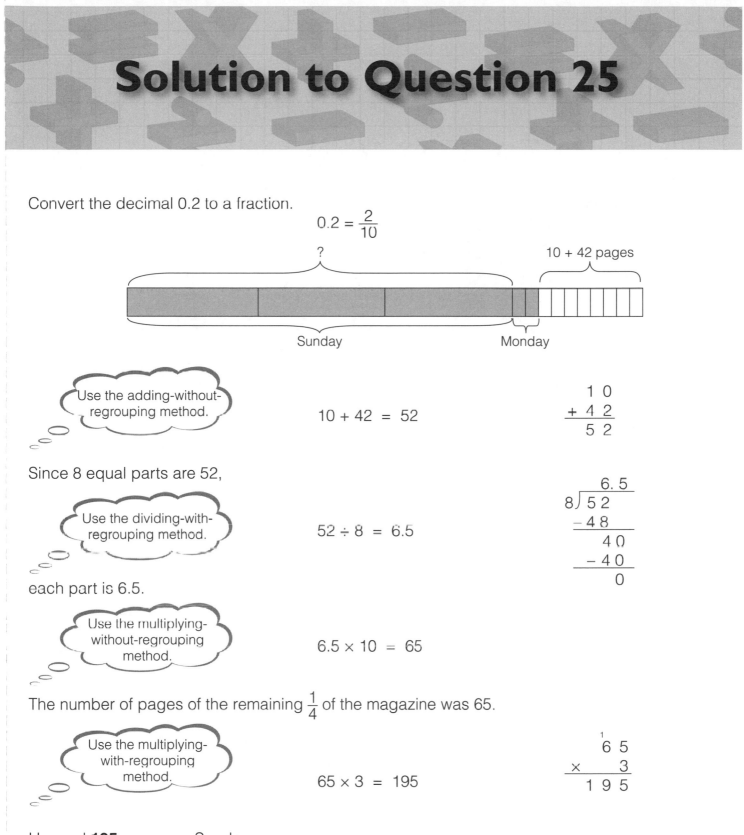

$$0.2 = \frac{2}{10}$$

Sunday   Monday

10 + 42 pages

Use the adding-without-regrouping method.

$$10 + 42 = 52$$

$$\begin{array}{r} 1\ 0 \\ +\ 4\ 2 \\ \hline 5\ 2 \end{array}$$

Since 8 equal parts are 52,

Use the dividing-with-regrouping method.

$$52 \div 8 = 6.5$$

$$\begin{array}{r} 6.\ 5 \\ 8\overline{)5\ 2} \\ -4\ 8 \\ \hline 4\ 0 \\ -4\ 0 \\ \hline 0 \end{array}$$

each part is 6.5.

Use the multiplying-without-regrouping method.

$$6.5 \times 10 = 65$$

The number of pages of the remaining $\frac{1}{4}$ of the magazine was 65.

Use the multiplying-with-regrouping method.

$$65 \times 3 = 195$$

$$\begin{array}{r} {}^{1}6\ 5 \\ \times\qquad 3 \\ \hline 1\ 9\ 5 \end{array}$$

He read **195** pages on Sunday.

Answer: __**195 pages**__

Solution to Question 26

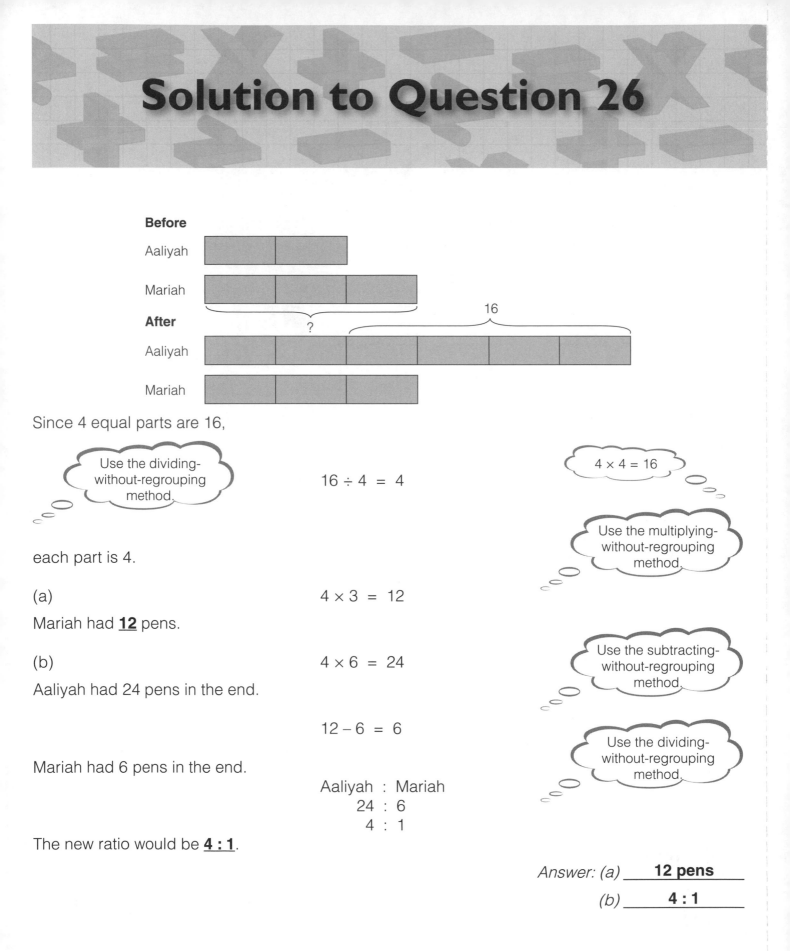

Before

Aaliyah

Mariah

After

Aaliyah

Mariah

16

?

Since 4 equal parts are 16,

Use the dividing-without-regrouping method.

$16 \div 4 = 4$

$4 \times 4 = 16$

Use the multiplying-without-regrouping method.

each part is 4.

(a)

$4 \times 3 = 12$

Mariah had **12** pens.

(b)

$4 \times 6 = 24$

Aaliyah had 24 pens in the end.

Use the subtracting-without-regrouping method.

$12 - 6 = 6$

Use the dividing-without-regrouping method.

Mariah had 6 pens in the end.

Aaliyah : Mariah
24 : 6
4 : 1

The new ratio would be **4 : 1**.

Answer: (a) _____ **12 pens** _____

(b) _____ **4 : 1** _____

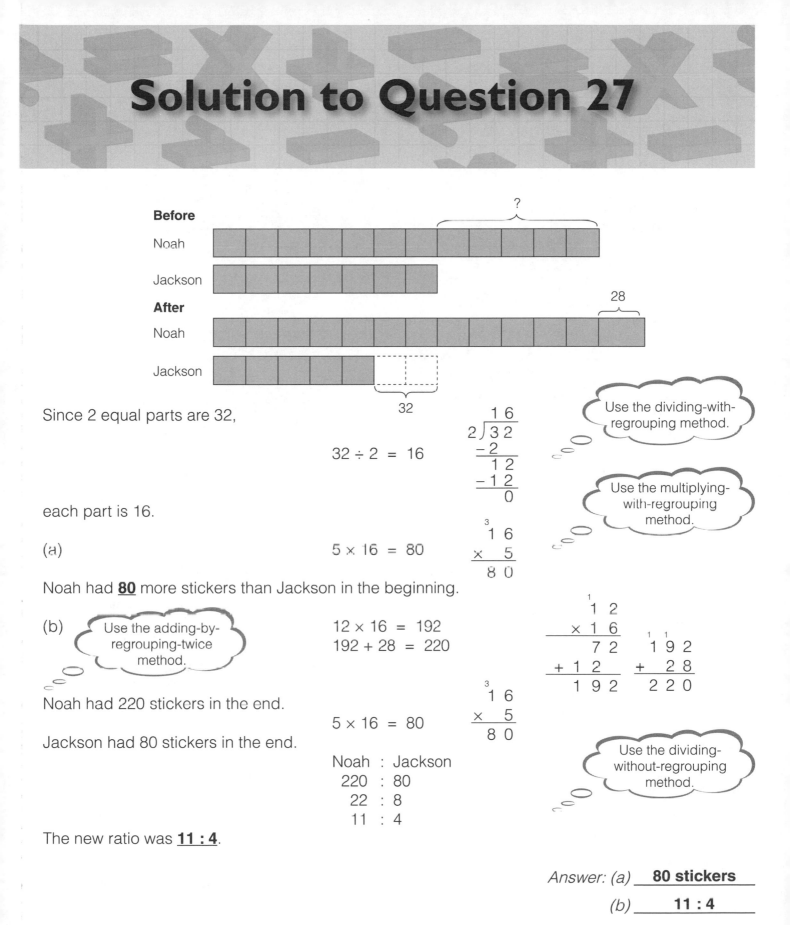

Before

Noah

Jackson

After

Noah

28

Jackson

32

Since 2 equal parts are 32,

$$32 \div 2 = 16$$

$$
\begin{array}{r}
1\ 6 \\
2\overline{)3\ 2} \\
-2 \\
\hline
1\ 2 \\
-1\ 2 \\
\hline
0
\end{array}
$$

Use the dividing-with-regrouping method.

each part is 16.

(a)

$$5 \times 16 = 80$$

$$
\begin{array}{r}
{}^{3}\ 1\ 6 \\
\times\ \ \ 5 \\
\hline
8\ 0
\end{array}
$$

Use the multiplying-with-regrouping method.

Noah had **80** more stickers than Jackson in the beginning.

(b) Use the adding-by-regrouping-twice method.

$$12 \times 16 = 192$$
$$192 + 28 = 220$$

$$
\begin{array}{r}
{}^{1}\ 1\ 2 \\
\times\ 1\ 6 \\
\hline
7\ 2 \\
+\ 1\ 2 \\
\hline
1\ 9\ 2
\end{array}
\qquad
\begin{array}{r}
{}^{1}\ {}^{1} \\
1\ 9\ 2 \\
+\ \ 2\ 8 \\
\hline
2\ 2\ 0
\end{array}
$$

Noah had 220 stickers in the end.

Jackson had 80 stickers in the end.

$$5 \times 16 = 80$$

$$
\begin{array}{r}
{}^{3}\ 1\ 6 \\
\times\ \ \ 5 \\
\hline
8\ 0
\end{array}
$$

Noah : Jackson
220 : 80
22 : 8
11 : 4

Use the dividing-without-regrouping method.

The new ratio was **11 : 4**.

Answer: (a) __**80 stickers**__

(b) __**11 : 4**__

Solution to Question 28

Before

Alex

Ellie

After

72

Alex

Ellie

?

Since 9 equal parts are 72,

Use the multiplying-without-regrouping method.

$72 \div 9 = 8$

$9 \times 8 = 72$

each part is 8.

(a)

$8 \times 4 = 32$

Ellie had **32** beads.

(b)

$8 \times 12 = 96$

Use the multiplying-without-regrouping method.

$$\begin{array}{r} {}^{1}\,2 \\ \times\ \ 8 \\ \hline 9\ 6 \end{array}$$

Use the subtracting-without-regrouping method.

$96 - 80 = 16$

$$\begin{array}{r} 9\ 6 \\ -\ 8\ 0 \\ \hline 1\ 6 \end{array}$$

Alex had 16 beads in the end.

Use with dividing-with-regrouping method.

Ellie : Alex
32 : 16
2 : 1

The new ratio would be **2 : 1**.

Answer: (a) ___**32 beads**___

(b) ___**2 : 1**___

Solution to Question 29

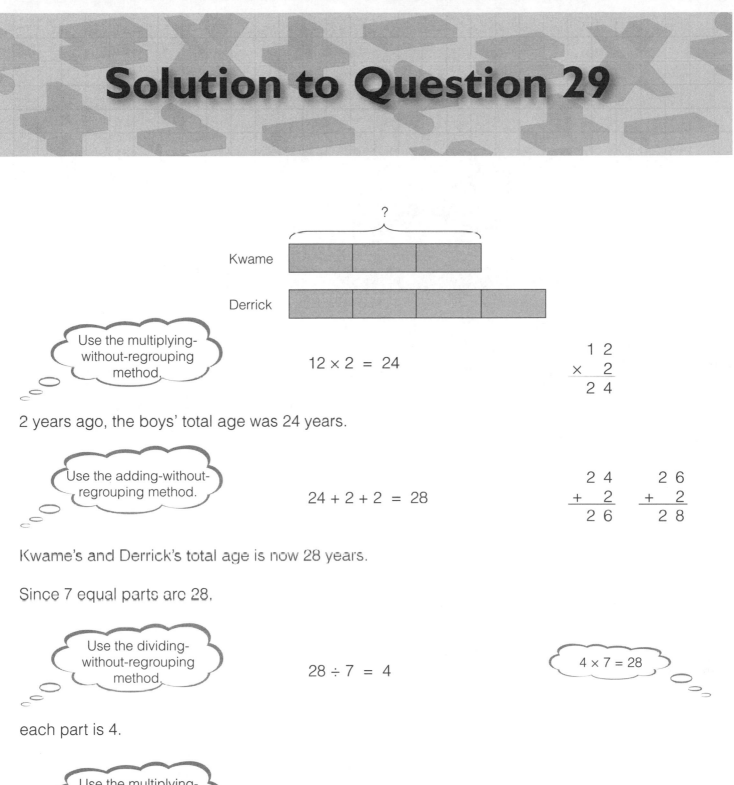

Kwame

Derrick

> Use the multiplying-without-regrouping method.

$12 \times 2 = 24$

$$\begin{array}{r} 1\ 2 \\ \times\quad 2 \\ \hline 2\ 4 \end{array}$$

2 years ago, the boys' total age was 24 years.

> Use the adding-without-regrouping method.

$24 + 2 + 2 = 28$

$$\begin{array}{r} 2\ 4 \\ +\quad 2 \\ \hline 2\ 6 \end{array} \qquad \begin{array}{r} 2\ 6 \\ +\quad 2 \\ \hline 2\ 8 \end{array}$$

Kwame's and Derrick's total age is now 28 years.

Since 7 equal parts are 28,

> Use the dividing-without-regrouping method.

$28 \div 7 = 4$

> $4 \times 7 = 28$

each part is 4.

> Use the multiplying-without-regrouping method.

$4 \times 3 = 12$

Kwame is **12** years old now.

Answer: **12 years old**

Solution to Question 30

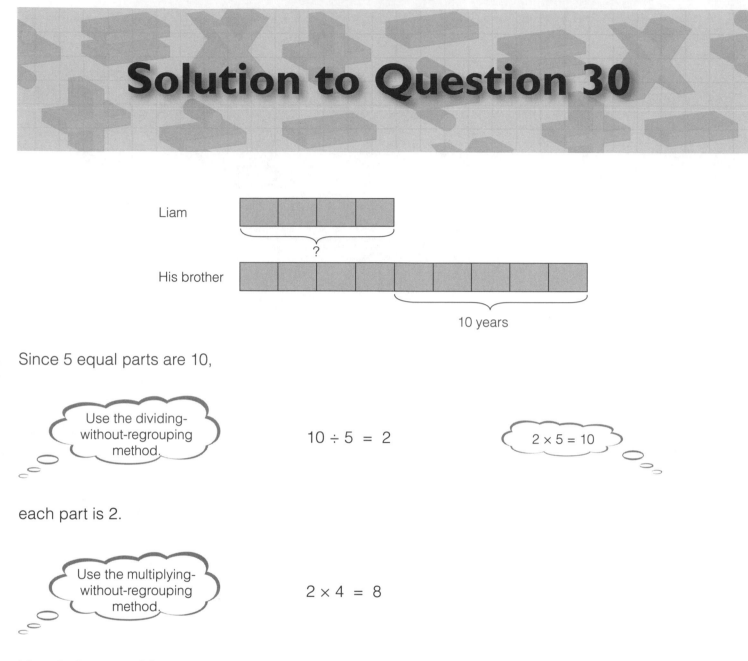

Liam

His brother

?

10 years

Since 5 equal parts are 10,

Use the dividing-without-regrouping method.

$10 \div 5 = 2$

$2 \times 5 = 10$

each part is 2.

Use the multiplying-without-regrouping method.

$2 \times 4 = 8$

Liam is **8** years old now.

Answer: __**8 years old**__

Solution to Question 31

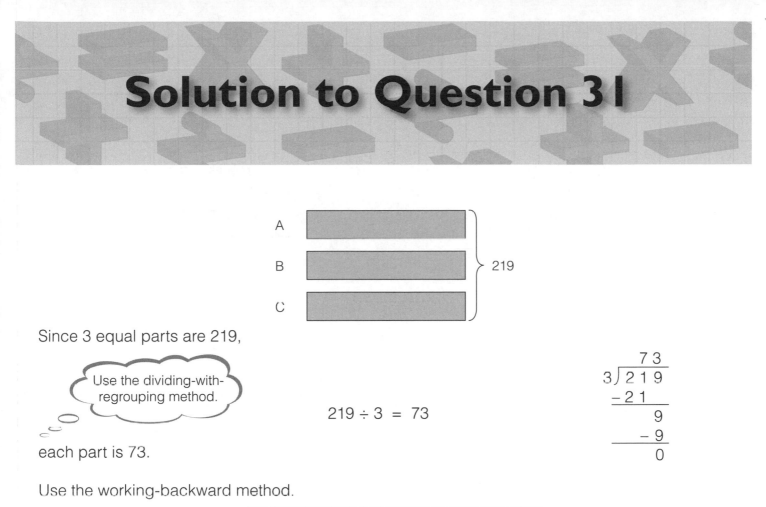

Since 3 equal parts are 219,

> Use the dividing-with-regrouping method.

$$219 \div 3 = 73$$

```
      7 3
  3 ) 2 1 9
     -2 1
        9
       -9
        0
```

each part is 73.

Use the working-backward method.

	Moved	**Received**
Container A	21	18
Container B	27	21
Container C	18	27

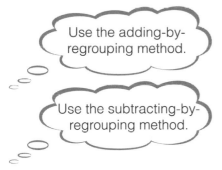

> Use the adding-by-regrouping method.

> Use the subtracting-by-regrouping method.

Container A $= 73 + 21 - 18 = 76$

Container B $= 73 + 27 - 21 = 79$

Container C $= 73 + 18 - 27 = 64$

There were **76** marbles in Container A, **79** marbles in Container B, and **64** marbles in Container C in the beginning.

Answer: **Container A: 76 marbles**
Container B: 79 marbles
Container C: 64 marbles

Solution to Question 32

(a)

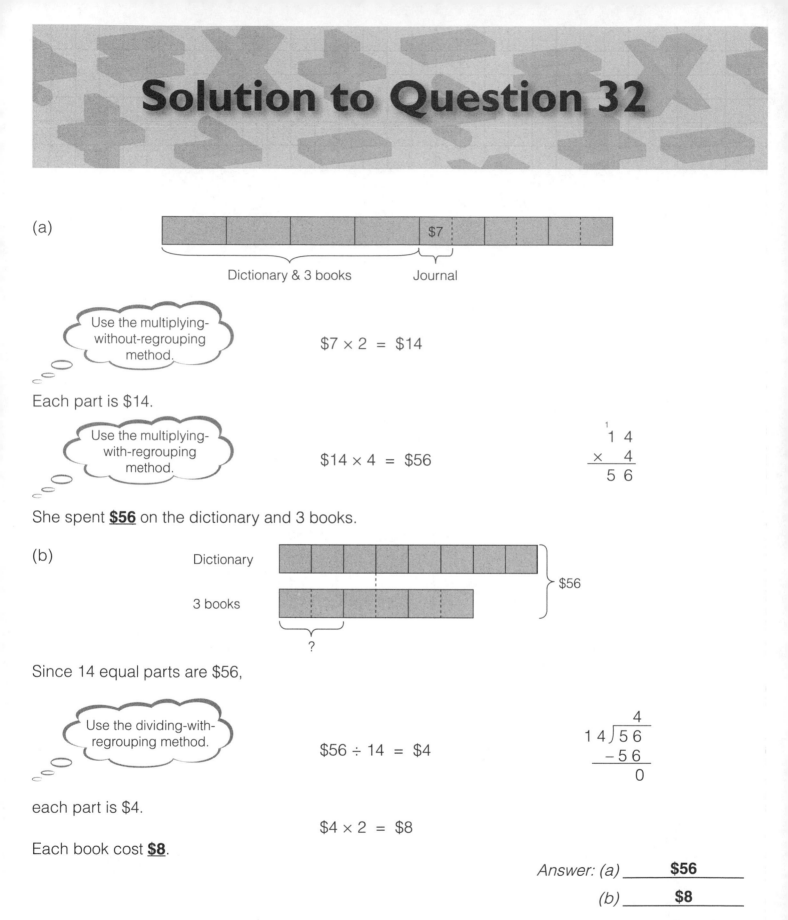

Dictionary & 3 books   Journal

Use the multiplying-without-regrouping method.

$7 × 2 = $14

Each part is $14.

Use the multiplying-with-regrouping method.

$14 × 4 = $56

$$
\begin{array}{r}
^{1}1\,4 \\
\times\ \ 4 \\
\hline
5\,6
\end{array}
$$

She spent **$56** on the dictionary and 3 books.

(b)

Dictionary

3 books

$56

?

Since 14 equal parts are $56,

Use the dividing-with-regrouping method.

$56 ÷ 14 = $4

$$
\begin{array}{r}
4 \\
14\,\overline{)\,56} \\
-5\,6 \\
\hline
0
\end{array}
$$

each part is $4.

$4 × 2 = $8

Each book cost **$8**.

Answer: (a) _____ **$56** _____

(b) _____ **$8** _____

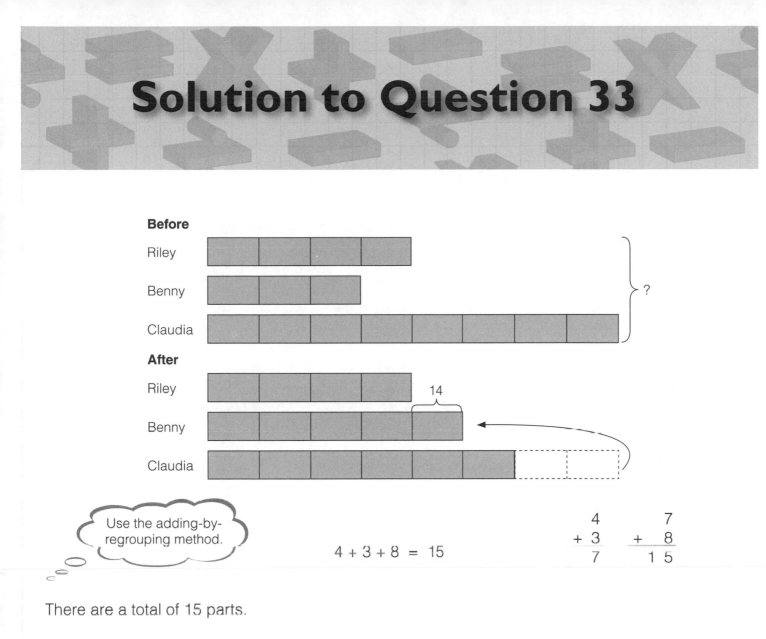

Before

Riley

Benny

Claudia

After

Riley

14

Benny

Claudia

Use the adding-by-regrouping method.

$4 + 3 + 8 = 15$

$$\begin{array}{r} 4 \\ + 3 \\ \hline 7 \end{array} \qquad \begin{array}{r} 7 \\ + 8 \\ \hline 1\,5 \end{array}$$

There are a total of 15 parts.

Since each part is 14,

Use the multiplying-with-regrouping method.

$14 \times 15 = 210$

$$\begin{array}{r} \overset{2}{1}\,5 \\ \times\ 1\,4 \\ \hline 6\,0 \\ +\ \overset{1}{1}\,5 \\ \hline 2\,1\,0 \end{array}$$

there are **210** peas altogether.

Answer: **210 peas**

Solution to Question 34

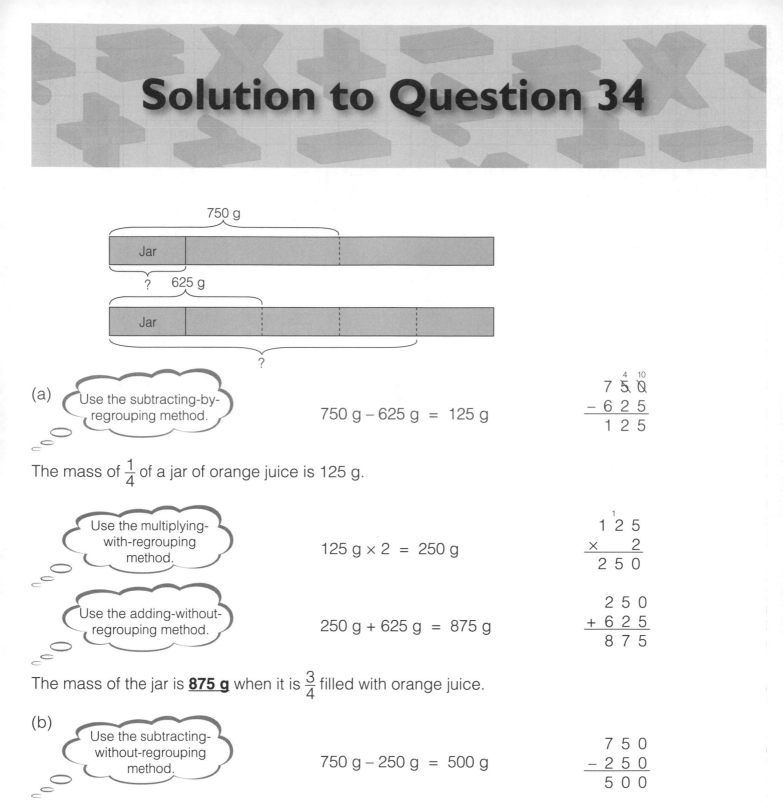

(a)
Use the subtracting-by-regrouping method.

$$750 \text{ g} - 625 \text{ g} = 125 \text{ g}$$

$$
\begin{array}{r}
7\,\overset{4}{\cancel{5}}\,\overset{10}{\cancel{0}} \\
-\ 6\ 2\ 5 \\
\hline
1\ 2\ 5
\end{array}
$$

The mass of $\frac{1}{4}$ of a jar of orange juice is 125 g.

Use the multiplying-with-regrouping method.

$$125 \text{ g} \times 2 = 250 \text{ g}$$

$$
\begin{array}{r}
1\,\overset{1}{2}\,5 \\
\times\quad\ 2 \\
\hline
2\ 5\ 0
\end{array}
$$

Use the adding-without-regrouping method.

$$250 \text{ g} + 625 \text{ g} = 875 \text{ g}$$

$$
\begin{array}{r}
2\ 5\ 0 \\
+\ 6\ 2\ 5 \\
\hline
8\ 7\ 5
\end{array}
$$

The mass of the jar is **875 g** when it is $\frac{3}{4}$ filled with orange juice.

(b)
Use the subtracting-without-regrouping method.

$$750 \text{ g} - 250 \text{ g} = 500 \text{ g}$$

$$
\begin{array}{r}
7\ 5\ 0 \\
-\ 2\ 5\ 0 \\
\hline
5\ 0\ 0
\end{array}
$$

The mass of the jar is **500 g** when it is empty.

Answer: (a) ____**875 g**____

(b) ____**500 g**____

Solution to Question 35

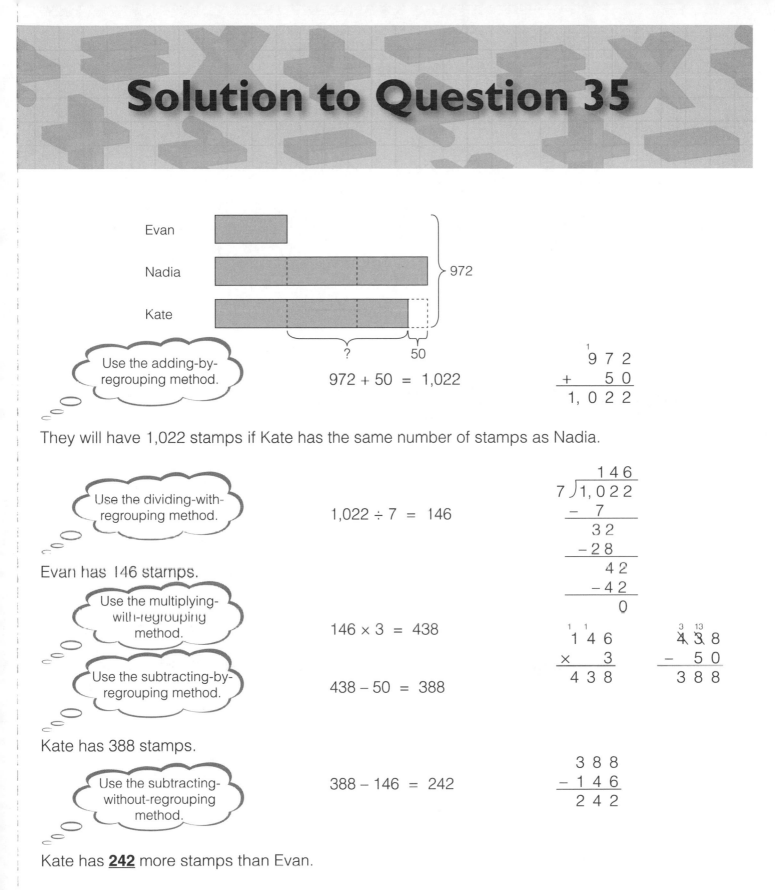

Evan

Nadia

Kate

} 972

? 50

Use the adding-by-regrouping method.

$972 + 50 = 1,022$

$$\begin{array}{r} \overset{1}{9}\,7\,2 \\ +\quad 5\,0 \\ \hline 1,0\,2\,2 \end{array}$$

They will have 1,022 stamps if Kate has the same number of stamps as Nadia.

Use the dividing-with-regrouping method.

$1,022 \div 7 = 146$

$$\begin{array}{r} 146 \\ 7\overline{)1,022} \\ -7 \\ \hline 32 \\ -28 \\ \hline 42 \\ -42 \\ \hline 0 \end{array}$$

Evan has 146 stamps.

Use the multiplying-with-regrouping method.

$146 \times 3 = 438$

Use the subtracting-by-regrouping method.

$438 - 50 = 388$

$$\begin{array}{r} \overset{1}{1}\overset{1}{4}\,6 \\ \times\quad 3 \\ \hline 4\,3\,8 \end{array} \qquad \begin{array}{r} \overset{3}{4}\overset{13}{3}\,8 \\ -\quad 5\,0 \\ \hline 3\,8\,8 \end{array}$$

Kate has 388 stamps.

Use the subtracting-without-regrouping method.

$388 - 146 = 242$

$$\begin{array}{r} 3\,8\,8 \\ -1\,4\,6 \\ \hline 2\,4\,2 \end{array}$$

Kate has **242** more stamps than Evan.

Answer: **242 more stamps**

Solution to Question 36

Use the adding-by-regrouping method.

$24 + 18 = 42$

$$\begin{array}{r} \overset{1}{2}\ 4 \\ +\ 1\ 8 \\ \hline 4\ 2 \end{array}$$

There are 42 students in the class.

Use the dividing-without-regrouping method.

Number of boys	:	Total number of students	
18	:	42	$6 \times 3 = 18$
3	:	7	$6 \times 7 = 42$

The ratio of the number of boys to the total number of students in the class is **3 : 7**.

Answer: _____**3 : 7**_____

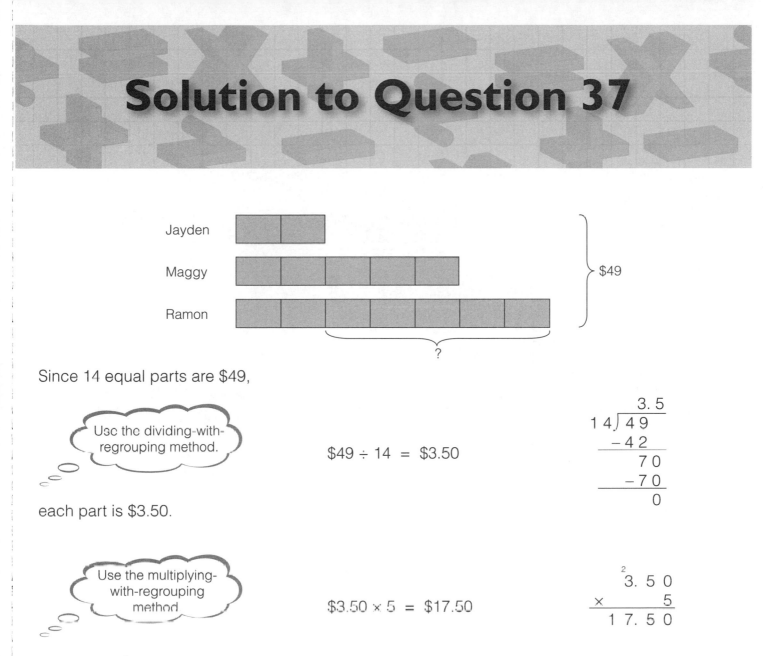

Since 14 equal parts are $49,

Use the dividing-with-regrouping method.

$49 ÷ 14 = $3.50

$$
\begin{array}{r}
3.\,5 \\
14\overline{\smash{)}49} \\
-42 \\
\hline
70 \\
-70 \\
\hline
0
\end{array}
$$

each part is $3.50.

Use the multiplying-with-regrouping method

$3.50 × 5 = $17.50

$$
\begin{array}{r}
{}^{2}\,3.\,5\,0 \\
\times \qquad 5 \\
\hline
17.\,5\,0
\end{array}
$$

Ramon got **$17.50** more than Jayden.

Answer: __$17.50 more__

Solution to Question 38

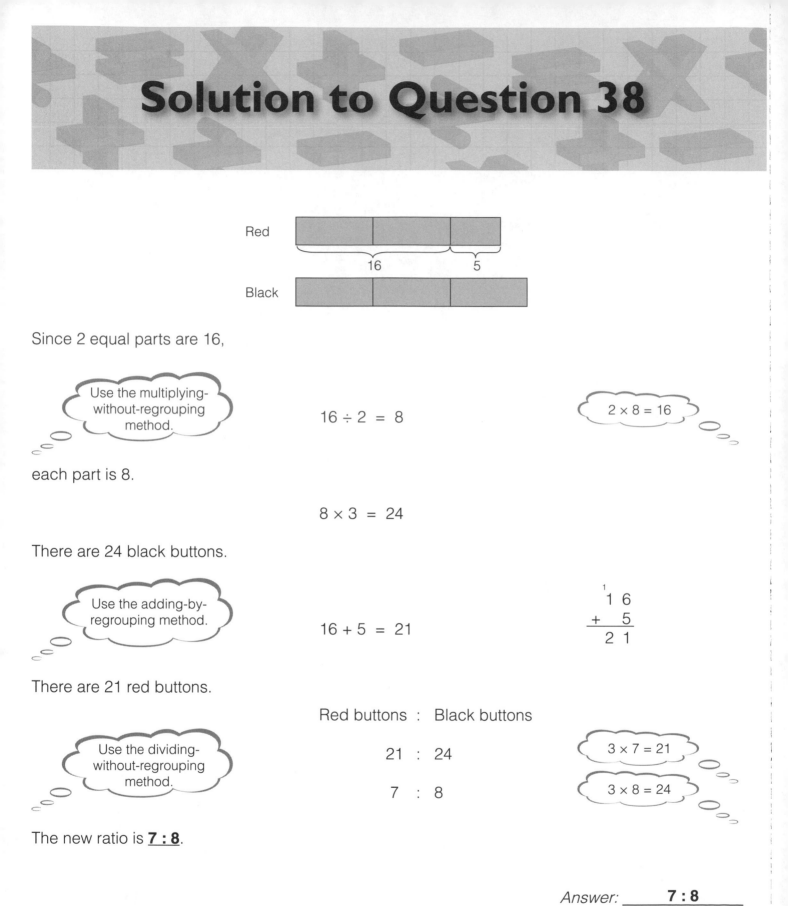

Red

16   5

Black

Since 2 equal parts are 16,

Use the multiplying-without-regrouping method.

$16 \div 2 = 8$

$2 \times 8 = 16$

each part is 8.

$8 \times 3 = 24$

There are 24 black buttons.

Use the adding-by-regrouping method.

$16 + 5 = 21$

$$\begin{array}{r} {}^{1}1\ 6 \\ +\quad 5 \\ \hline 2\ 1 \end{array}$$

There are 21 red buttons.

Red buttons : Black buttons

Use the dividing-without-regrouping method.

21 : 24

7 : 8

$3 \times 7 = 21$

$3 \times 8 = 24$

The new ratio is **7 : 8**.

Answer: **7 : 8**

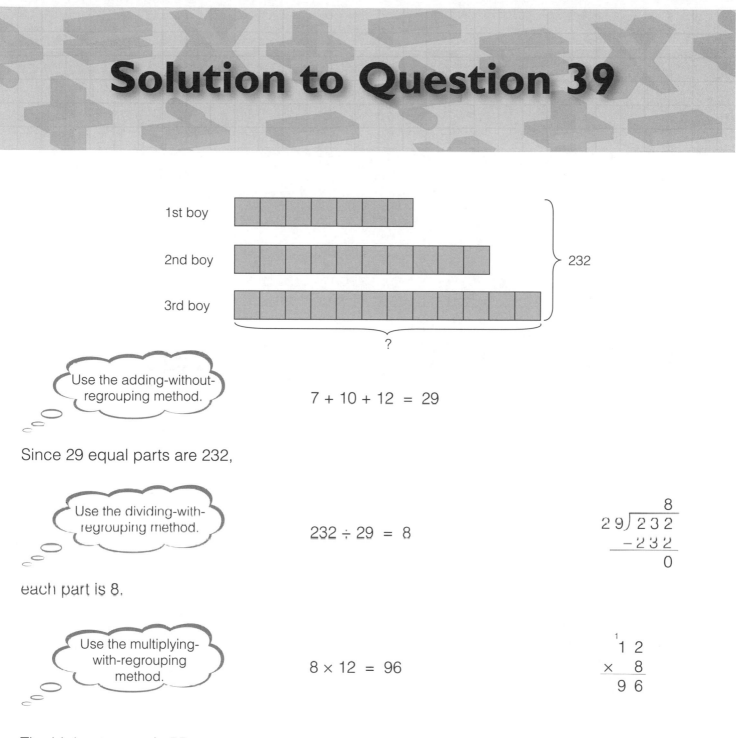

1st boy

2nd boy

3rd boy

232

?

Use the adding-without-regrouping method.

$7 + 10 + 12 = 29$

Since 29 equal parts are 232,

Use the dividing-with-regrouping method.

$232 \div 29 = 8$

$$\begin{array}{r} 8 \\ 29{\overline{\smash{\big)}\,232}} \\ \underline{-232} \\ 0 \end{array}$$

each part is 8.

Use the multiplying-with-regrouping method.

$8 \times 12 = 96$

$$\begin{array}{r} {}^1 1\;2 \\ \times\quad 8 \\ \hline 9\;6 \end{array}$$

The highest score is **96**.

Answer: ___**96 points**___

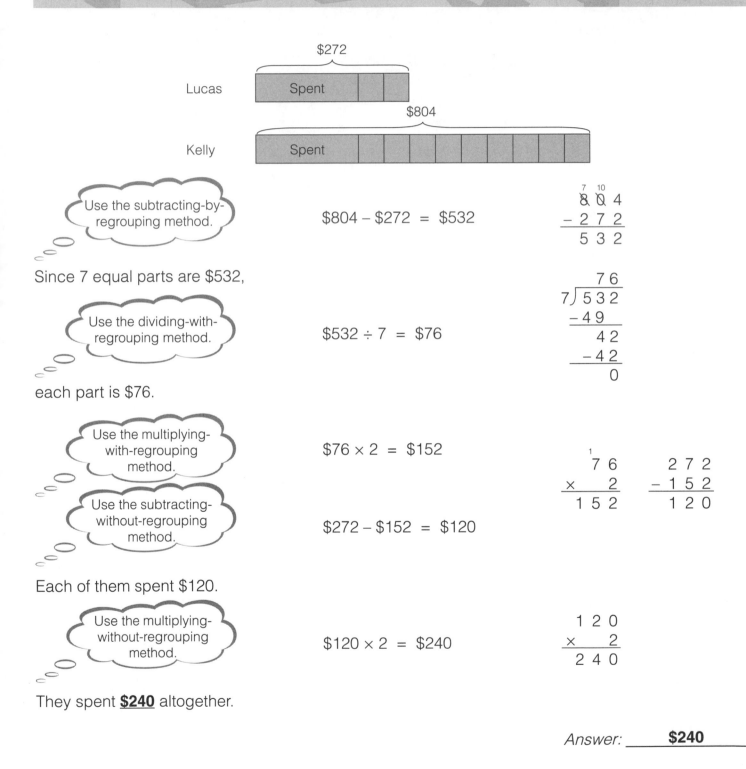

$272

Lucas | Spent

$804

Kelly | Spent

Use the subtracting-by-regrouping method.

$804 − $272 = $532

$$\begin{array}{r} {}^{7}\!\!\!\not{8}\ {}^{10}\!\!\!\not{0}\ 4 \\ -\ 2\ 7\ 2 \\ \hline 5\ 3\ 2 \end{array}$$

Since 7 equal parts are $532,

Use the dividing-with-regrouping method.

$532 ÷ 7 = $76

$$\begin{array}{r} 7\ 6 \\ 7\overline{)5\ 3\ 2} \\ -4\ 9 \\ \hline 4\ 2 \\ -4\ 2 \\ \hline 0 \end{array}$$

each part is $76.

Use the multiplying-with-regrouping method.

$76 × 2 = $152

Use the subtracting-without-regrouping method.

$272 − $152 = $120

$$\begin{array}{r} {}^{1} \\ 7\ 6 \\ \times\ \ \ 2 \\ \hline 1\ 5\ 2 \end{array} \qquad \begin{array}{r} 2\ 7\ 2 \\ -\ 1\ 5\ 2 \\ \hline 1\ 2\ 0 \end{array}$$

Each of them spent $120.

Use the multiplying-without-regrouping method.

$120 × 2 = $240

$$\begin{array}{r} 1\ 2\ 0 \\ \times\ \ \ \ 2 \\ \hline 2\ 4\ 0 \end{array}$$

They spent **$240** altogether.

Answer: _____**$240**_____

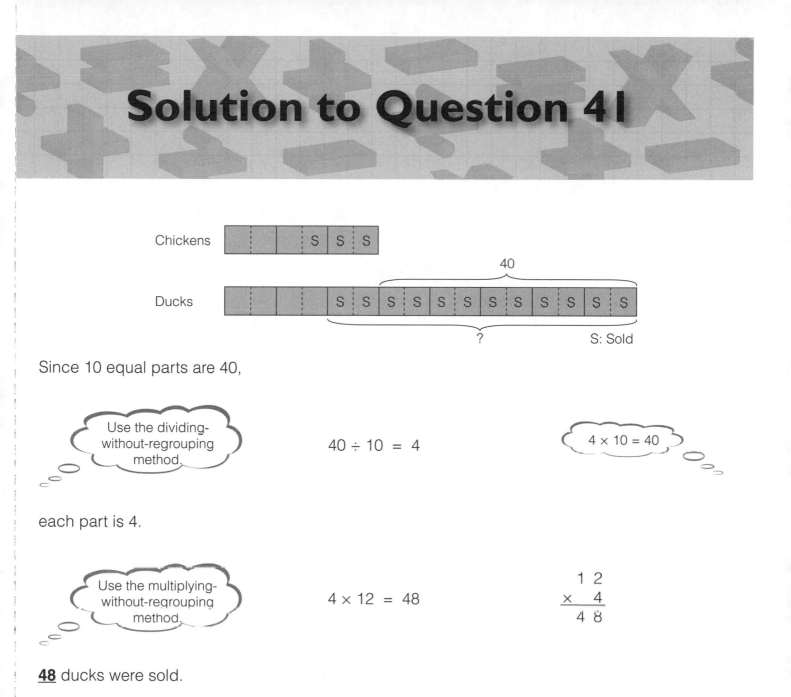

Chickens

40

Ducks

?   S: Sold

Since 10 equal parts are 40,

Use the dividing-without-regrouping method.

$$40 \div 10 = 4$$

$4 \times 10 = 40$

each part is 4.

Use the multiplying-without-regrouping method.

$$4 \times 12 = 48$$

$$\begin{array}{r} 1\ 2 \\ \times\quad 4 \\ \hline 4\ 8 \end{array}$$

48 ducks were sold.

Answer: __**48 ducks**__

Solution to Question 42

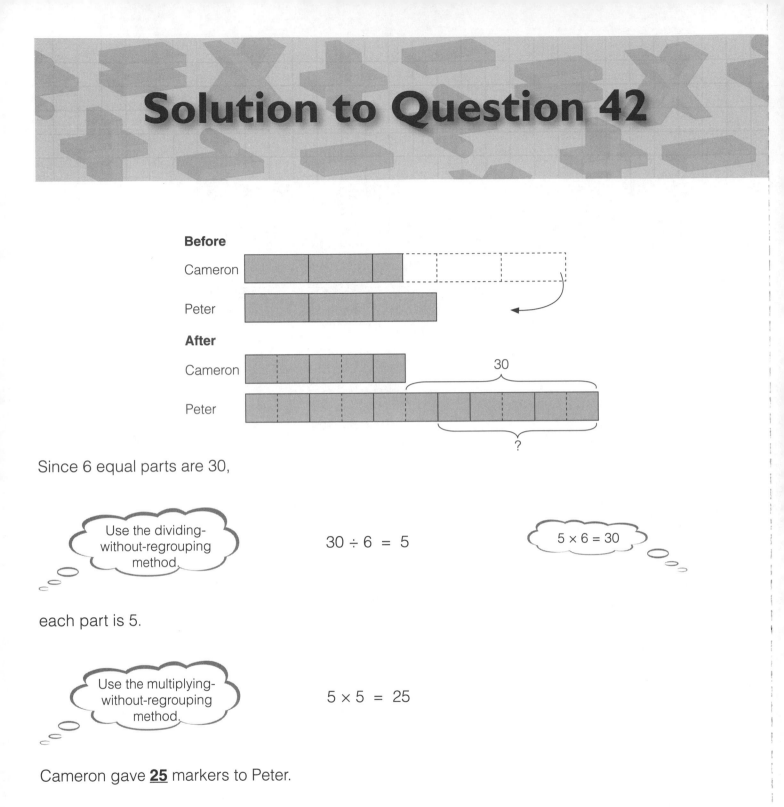

Before

Cameron

Peter

After

Cameron

30

Peter

?

Since 6 equal parts are 30,

Use the dividing-without-regrouping method.

$30 \div 6 = 5$

$5 \times 6 = 30$

each part is 5.

Use the multiplying-without-regrouping method.

$5 \times 5 = 25$

Cameron gave **25** markers to Peter.

Answer: __**25 markers**__

Solution to Question 43

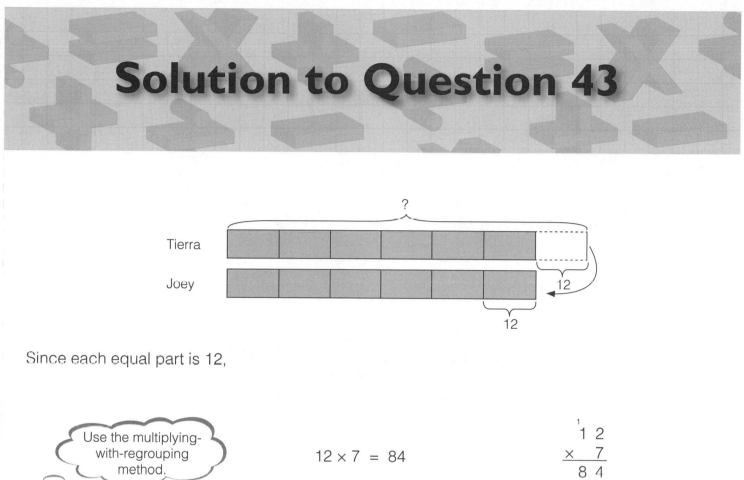

Since each equal part is 12,

Use the multiplying-with-regrouping method.

$$12 \times 7 = 84$$

$$\begin{array}{r} \overset{1}{1}\,2 \\ \times\quad 7 \\ \hline 8\,4 \end{array}$$

Tierra had **84** stamps in the beginning.

Answer: __**84 stamps**__

Solution to Question 44

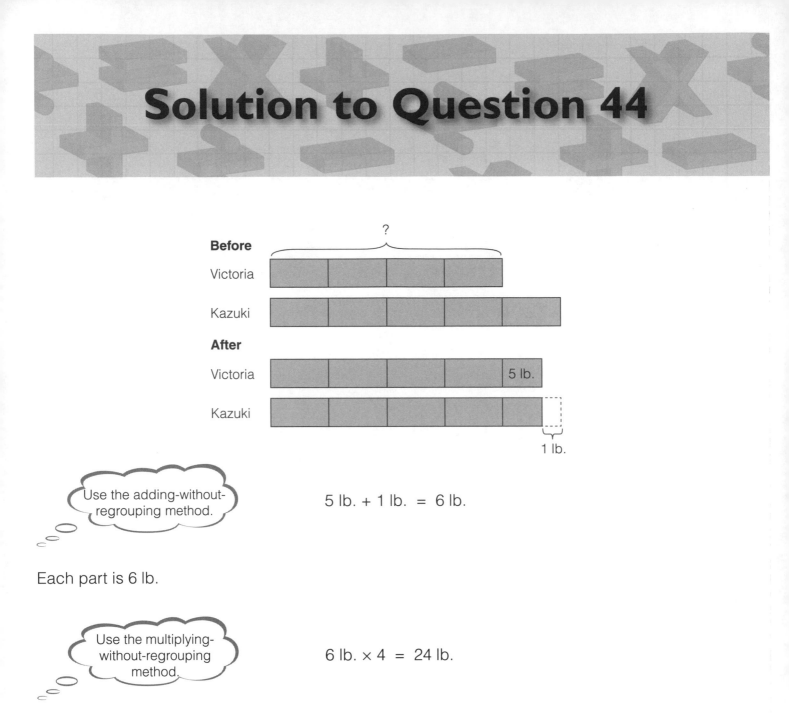

Before

?

Victoria

Kazuki

After

Victoria   5 lb.

Kazuki

1 lb.

Use the adding-without-regrouping method.

$$5 \text{ lb.} + 1 \text{ lb.} = 6 \text{ lb.}$$

Each part is 6 lb.

Use the multiplying-without-regrouping method.

$$6 \text{ lb.} \times 4 = 24 \text{ lb.}$$

Victoria's original weight was **24 lb.**

Answer: **24 lb.**

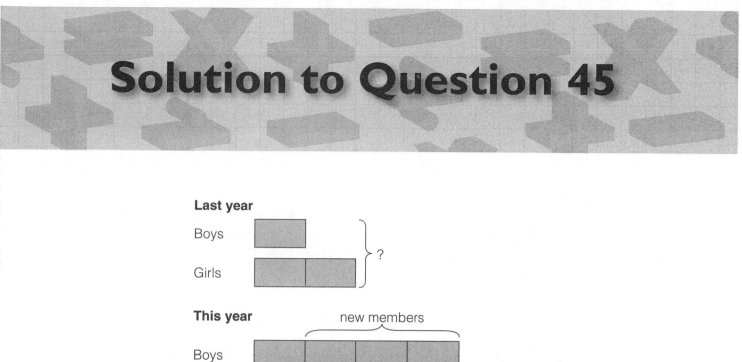

Last year

Boys

Girls

?

This year

new members

Boys

Girls

new members

There are 70 new members this year.

Since 7 equal parts are 70,

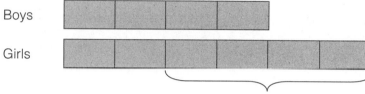

Use the dividing-without-regrouping method.

$$70 \div 7 = 10$$

$$7 \times 10 = 70$$

each part is 10.

Use the multiplying-without-regrouping method.

$$10 \times 3 = 30$$

There were **30** members in the computer club last year.

Answer: **30 members**

Solution to Question 46

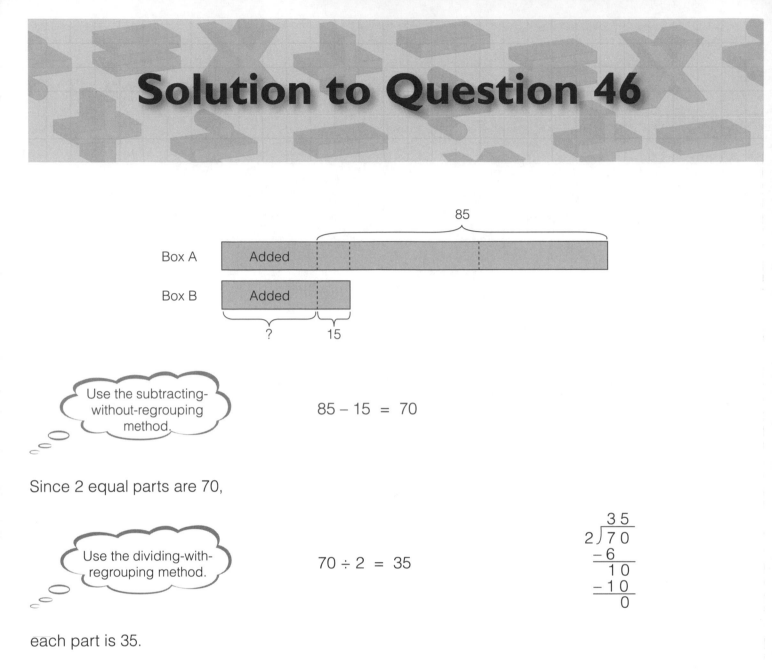

85 − 15 = 70

Since 2 equal parts are 70,

70 ÷ 2 = 35

each part is 35.

35 − 15 = 20

20 erasers were added to each box.

Answer: **20 erasers**

Solution to Question 47

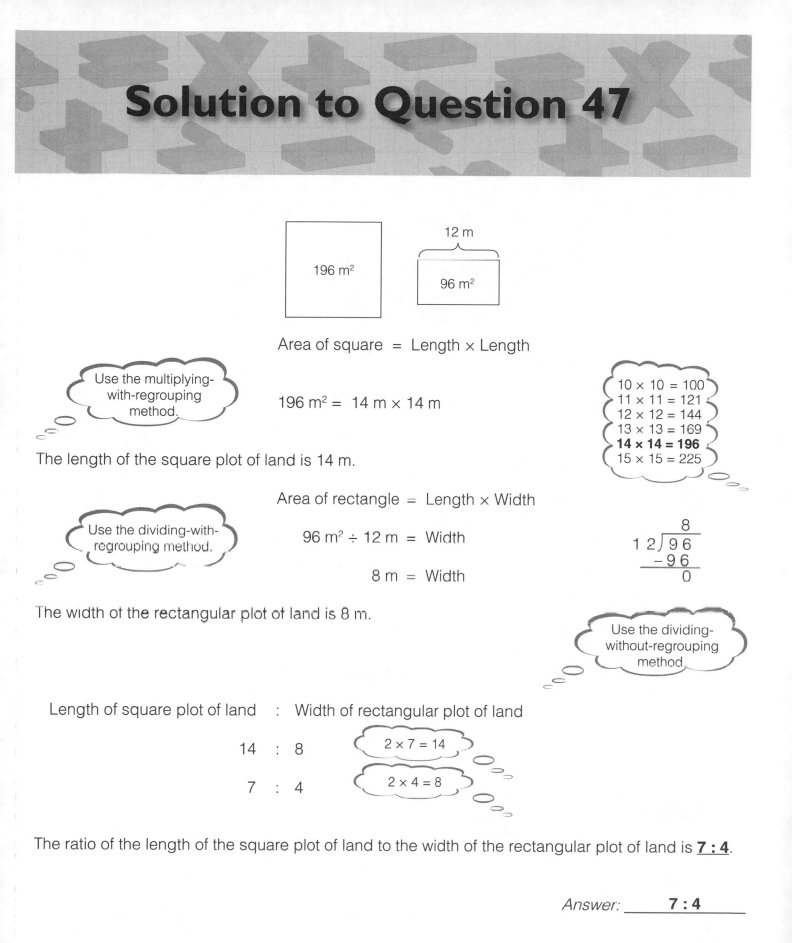

196 m²

12 m

96 m²

Area of square = Length × Length

> Use the multiplying-with-regrouping method.

196 m² = 14 m × 14 m

> 10 × 10 = 100
> 11 × 11 = 121
> 12 × 12 = 144
> 13 × 13 = 169
> **14 × 14 = 196**
> 15 × 15 = 225

The length of the square plot of land is 14 m.

Area of rectangle = Length × Width

> Use the dividing-with-regrouping method.

96 m² ÷ 12 m = Width

8 m = Width

$$\begin{array}{r} 8 \\ 12\overline{)96} \\ -96 \\ \hline 0 \end{array}$$

The width of the rectangular plot of land is 8 m.

> Use the dividing-without-regrouping method.

Length of square plot of land : Width of rectangular plot of land

14 : 8

7 : 4

> 2 × 7 = 14

> 2 × 4 = 8

The ratio of the length of the square plot of land to the width of the rectangular plot of land is **7 : 4**.

Answer: _____ **7 : 4** _____

Solution to Question 48

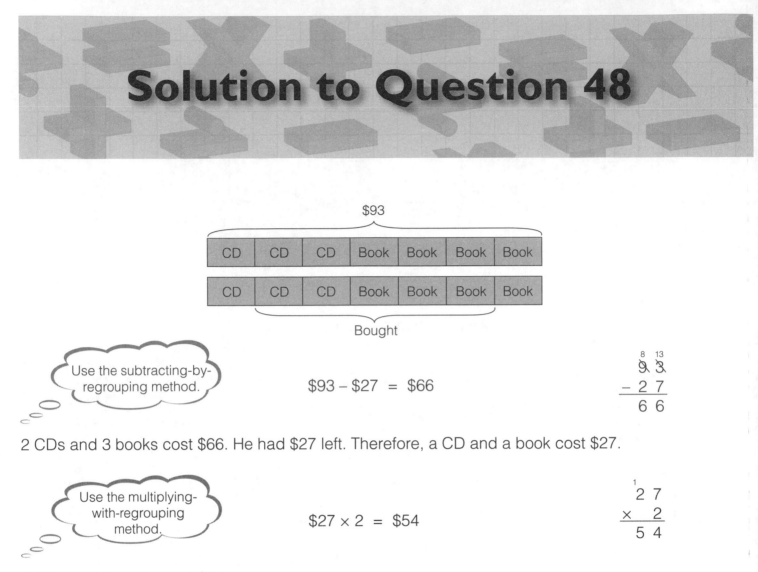

$93

CD	CD	CD	Book	Book	Book	Book

CD	CD	CD	Book	Book	Book	Book

Bought

Use the subtracting-by-regrouping method.

$93 − $27 = $66

$$\begin{array}{r} {}^{8}\,{}^{13}\\ \cancel{9}\ \cancel{3}\\ -\ 2\ 7\\ \hline 6\ 6 \end{array}$$

2 CDs and 3 books cost $66. He had $27 left. Therefore, a CD and a book cost $27.

Use the multiplying-with-regrouping method.

$27 × 2 = $54

$$\begin{array}{r} {}^{1}\\ 2\ 7\\ \times\ \ 2\\ \hline 5\ 4 \end{array}$$

2 CDs and 2 books cost $54.

Use the subtracting-without-regrouping method.

$66 − $54 = $12

$$\begin{array}{r} 6\ 6\\ -\ 5\ 4\\ \hline 1\ 2 \end{array}$$

Each book cost $12.

$27 − $12 = $15

$$\begin{array}{r} 2\ 7\\ -\ 1\ 2\\ \hline 1\ 5 \end{array}$$

Each CD cost **$15**.

Answer: _____**$15**_____

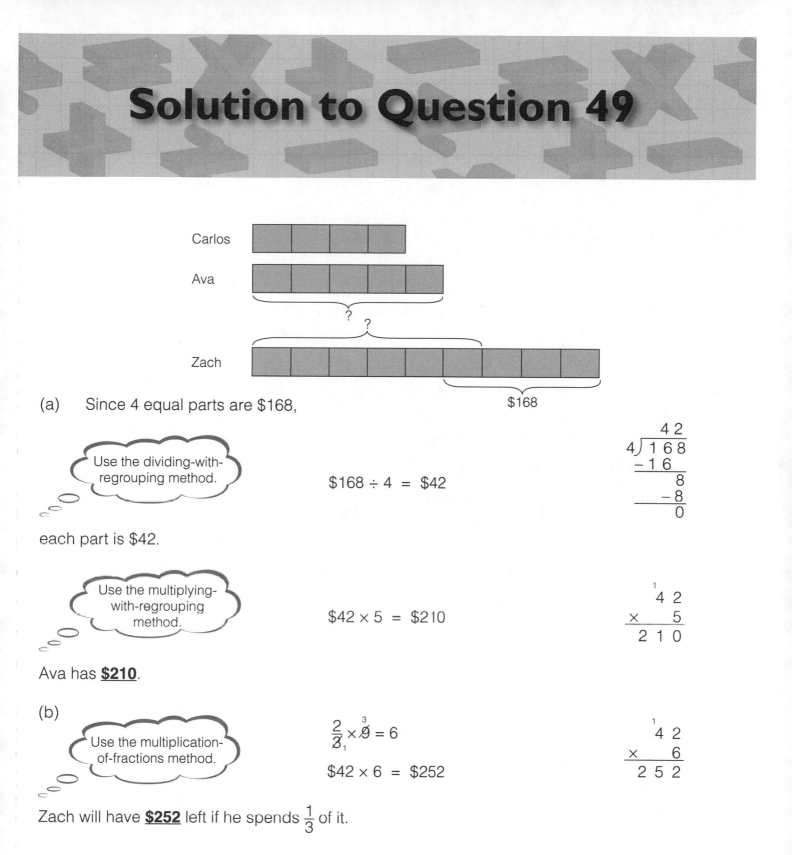

Carlos

Ava

? ?

Zach

$168

(a)   Since 4 equal parts are $168,

Use the dividing-with-regrouping method.

$168 \div 4 = $42

$$\begin{array}{r} 42 \\ 4\overline{)168} \\ -16 \\ \hline 8 \\ -8 \\ \hline 0 \end{array}$$

each part is $42.

Use the multiplying-with-regrouping method.

$42 \times 5 = $210

$$\begin{array}{r} \overset{1}{4}\,2 \\ \times 5 \\ \hline 2\,1\,0 \end{array}$$

Ava has **$210**.

(b)

Use the multiplication-of-fractions method.

$\dfrac{2}{\cancel{3}_1} \times \cancel{9}^{3} = 6$

$42 \times 6 = $252

$$\begin{array}{r} \overset{1}{4}\,2 \\ \times 6 \\ \hline 2\,5\,2 \end{array}$$

Zach will have **$252** left if he spends $\frac{1}{3}$ of it.

Answer: (a) _____**$210**_____

(b) _____**$252**_____

For every 25 watches Sarah sells,

> Use the multiplying-with-regrouping method.

$$\$4 \times 25 = \$100$$

$$\begin{array}{r} \overset{2}{2}\,5 \\ \times \quad 4 \\ \hline 1\,0\,0 \end{array}$$

> Use the adding-without-regrouping method.

$$\$100 + \$50 = \$150$$

she earns $150.

Using the guess-and-check method,

Number of watches	Amount of money she earns
25	$150
50	$150 + $150 = $300
75	**$300 + $150 = $450**
100	$450 + $150 = $600

Sarah had to sell 75 watches to earn $450.

> Use the subtracting-by-regrouping method.

$$\$506 - \$450 = \$56$$

> Use the dividing-with-regrouping method.

$$\$56 \div \$4 = 14$$

$$75 + 14 = 89$$

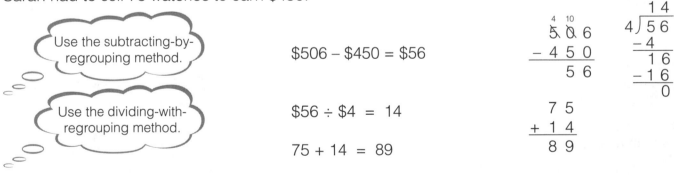

She sold **89** watches last month.

Answer: __**89 watches**__

Solution to Question 51

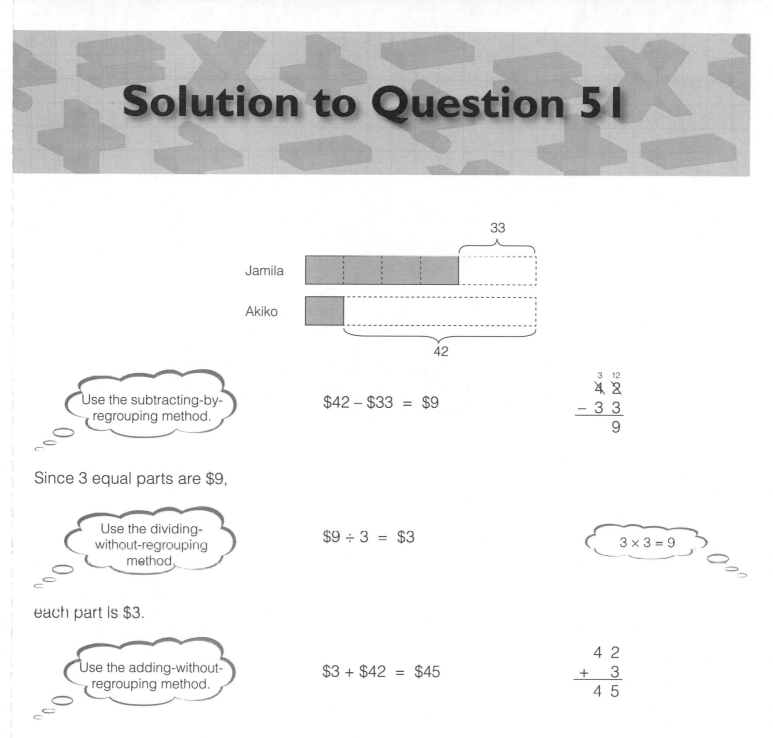

Use the subtracting-by-regrouping method.

$42 – $33 = $9

Since 3 equal parts are $9,

Use the dividing-without-regrouping method.

$9 ÷ 3 = $3

3 × 3 = 9

each part is $3.

Use the adding-without-regrouping method.

$3 + $42 = $45

Each of them had **$45** in the beginning.

Answer: <u>**$45**</u>

Solution to Question 52

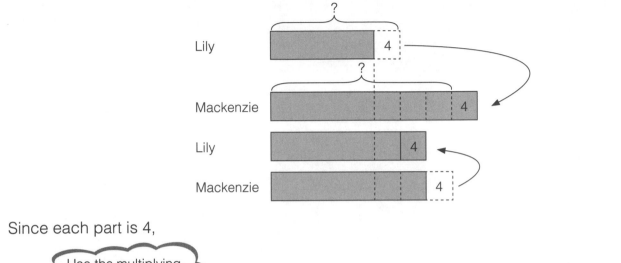

Since each part is 4,

Use the multiplying-without-regrouping method.

$$4 \times 4 = 16$$

half of Mackenzie's stamps would be 16 after Lily gave her 4 stamps.

$$16 + 4 = 20$$

Lily had **20** stamps.

Use the adding-by-regrouping method.

Use the multiplying-by-regrouping method.

$$16 \times 2 = 32$$

Use the subtracting-by-regrouping method.

$$32 - 4 = 28$$

Mackenzie had **28** stamps.

Answer: **Mackenzie: 28 stamps**
Lily: 20 stamps

Before

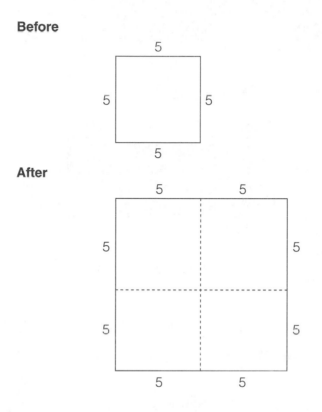

After

Since 10 people can sit on one side of the large square table,

Use the multiplying-without-regrouping method.

$$10 \times 4 = 40$$

40 people can sit around the large table.

Answer: __**40 people**__

Solution to Question 54

Use the adding-by-regrouping method.

$$240 + 260 = 500$$

$$\begin{array}{r} \overset{1}{2}\;4\;0 \\ +\;2\;6\;0 \\ \hline 5\;0\;0 \end{array}$$

Josh and Brianna had 500 seashells altogether.

After

Use the subtracting-by-regrouping method.

$$500 - 50 = 450$$

$$\begin{array}{r} \overset{4}{\cancel{5}}\;\overset{10}{\cancel{0}}\;0 \\ -\quad\;5\;0 \\ \hline 4\;5\;0 \end{array}$$

Since 2 equal parts are 450,

Use the dividing-with-regrouping method.

$$450 \div 2 = 225$$

$$\begin{array}{r} 225 \\ 2\overline{)450} \\ \underline{-4} \\ 5 \\ \underline{-4} \\ 10 \\ \underline{-10} \\ 0 \end{array}$$

Brianna should have 225 shells so that Josh has 50 more shells than her.

$$260 - 225 = 35$$

$$\begin{array}{r} 2\;\overset{5}{\cancel{6}}\;\overset{10}{\cancel{0}} \\ -\;2\;2\;5 \\ \hline 3\;5 \end{array}$$

Brianna gave **35** seashells to Josh.

Answer: __**35 seashells**__

Solution to Question 55

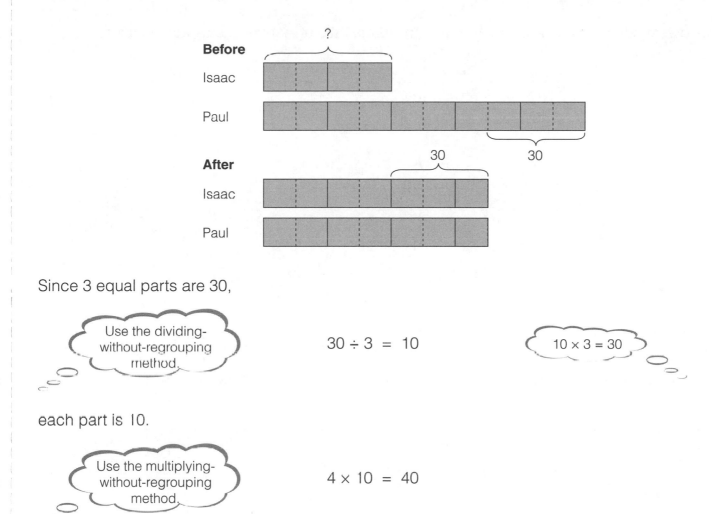

Since 3 equal parts are 30,

Use the dividing-without-regrouping method.

$$30 \div 3 = 10$$

10 × 3 = 30

each part is 10.

Use the multiplying-without-regrouping method.

$$4 \times 10 = 40$$

Isaac had **40** baseball cards in the beginning.

Answer: **40 baseball cards**

Solution to Question 56

Use the lowest common multiple of 7 and 3 to make the ratio of Hannah's savings the same.

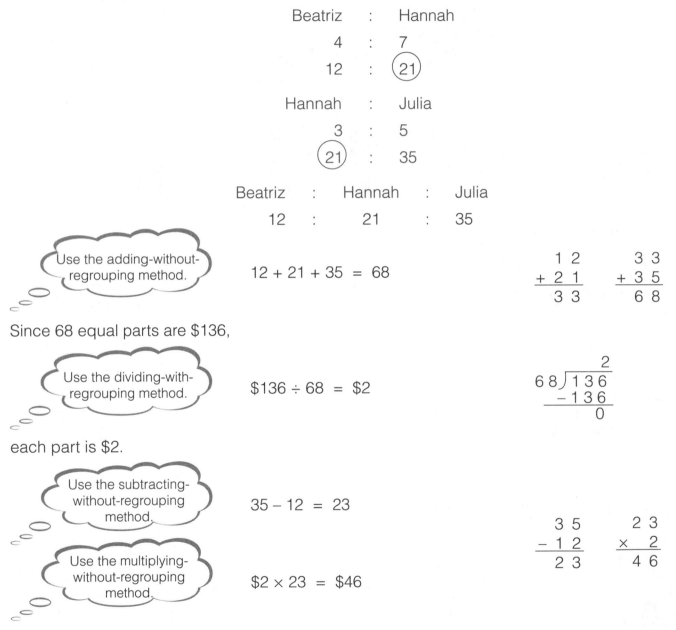

Beatriz   :   Hannah

4   :   7

12   :   ㉑

Hannah   :   Julia

3   :   5

㉑   :   35

Beatriz   :   Hannah   :   Julia

12   :   21   :   35

Use the adding-without-regrouping method.

$12 + 21 + 35 = 68$

$$\begin{array}{r} 1\ 2 \\ +\ 2\ 1 \\ \hline 3\ 3 \end{array} \qquad \begin{array}{r} 3\ 3 \\ +\ 3\ 5 \\ \hline 6\ 8 \end{array}$$

Since 68 equal parts are $136,

Use the dividing-with-regrouping method.

$\$136 \div 68 = \$2$

$$\begin{array}{r} 2 \\ 6\,8\,\overline{)1\,3\,6} \\ -1\,3\,6 \\ \hline 0 \end{array}$$

each part is $2.

Use the subtracting-without-regrouping method.

$35 - 12 = 23$

Use the multiplying-without-regrouping method.

$\$2 \times 23 = \$46$

$$\begin{array}{r} 3\ 5 \\ -\ 1\ 2 \\ \hline 2\ 3 \end{array} \qquad \begin{array}{r} 2\ 3 \\ \times\ \ \ 2 \\ \hline 4\ 6 \end{array}$$

Julia saved **$46** more than Beatriz.

Answer: **$46 more**

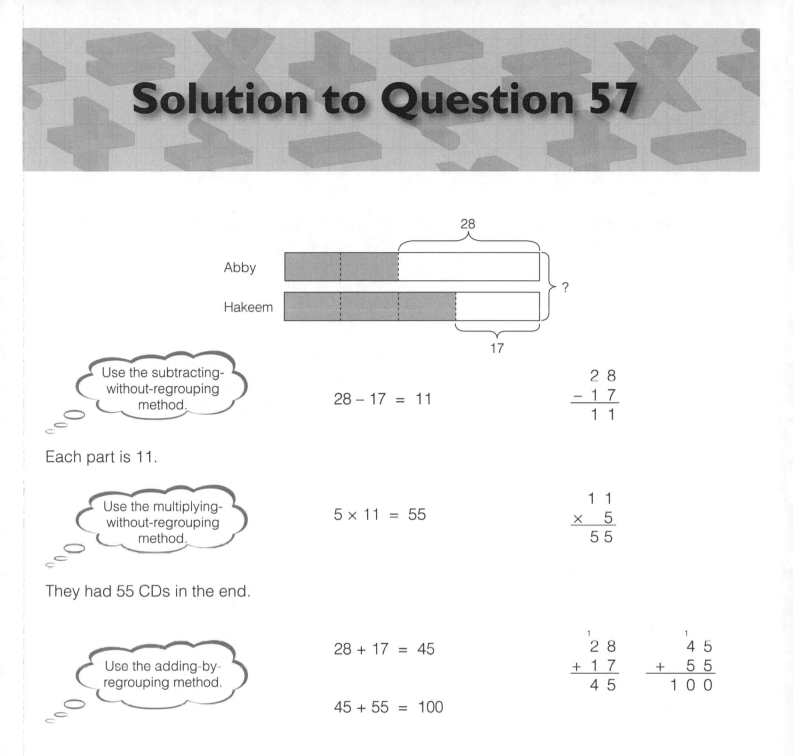

Use the subtracting-without-regrouping method.

$$28 - 17 = 11$$

$$\begin{array}{r} 2\ 8 \\ -\ 1\ 7 \\ \hline 1\ 1 \end{array}$$

Each part is 11.

Use the multiplying-without-regrouping method.

$$5 \times 11 = 55$$

$$\begin{array}{r} 1\ 1 \\ \times\quad 5 \\ \hline 5\ 5 \end{array}$$

They had 55 CDs in the end.

Use the adding-by-regrouping method.

$$28 + 17 = 45$$

$$45 + 55 = 100$$

$$\begin{array}{r} \overset{1}{2}\ 8 \\ +\ 1\ 7 \\ \hline 4\ 5 \end{array}\qquad \begin{array}{r} \overset{1}{4}\ 5 \\ +\ 5\ 5 \\ \hline 1\ 0\ 0 \end{array}$$

They had **100** CDs altogether in the beginning.

Answer: <u>**100 CDs**</u>

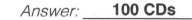

(a)   Use the lowest common multiple of 1 and 3 to make the ratio of SUVs the same.

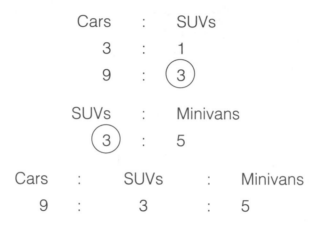

Cars : SUVs

3 : 1

9 : ③

SUVs : Minivans

③ : 5

Cars : SUVs : Minivans

9 : 3 : 5

The ratio of the number of cars to the number of SUVs to the number of minivans is **9 : 3 : 5**.

(b)   Since 5 equal parts are 20,

> Use the dividing-without-regrouping method.

$20 \div 5 = 4$

> $4 \times 5 = 20$

each part is 4.

> Use the adding-by-regrouping method.

$9 + 3 + 5 = 17$

$$\begin{array}{r} 9 \\ +\ \ 3 \\ \hline 1\ 2 \end{array} \qquad \begin{array}{r} 1\ 2 \\ +\ \ 5 \\ \hline 1\ 7 \end{array}$$

> Use the multiplying-with-regrouping method.

$17 \times 4 = 68$

$$\begin{array}{r} ^2\ \\ 1\ 7 \\ \times\ \ 4 \\ \hline 6\ 8 \end{array}$$

There are **68** vehicles altogether.

Answer: (a) _____ **9 : 3 : 5**

(b) _____ **68 vehicles**

Solution to Question 59

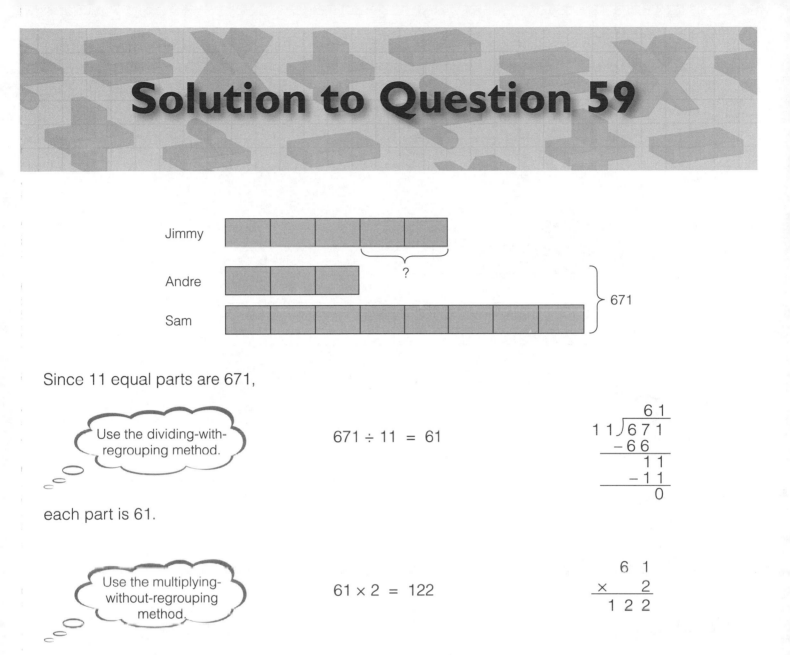

Since 11 equal parts are 671,

Use the dividing-with-regrouping method.

$671 \div 11 = 61$

```
      6 1
11 ⟌ 6 7 1
   − 6 6
      1 1
    − 1 1
         0
```

each part is 61.

Use the multiplying-without-regrouping method.

$61 \times 2 = 122$

```
    6 1
×     2
  1 2 2
```

Jimmy received **122** more pennies than Andre.

Answer: **122 more pennies**

Solution to Question 60

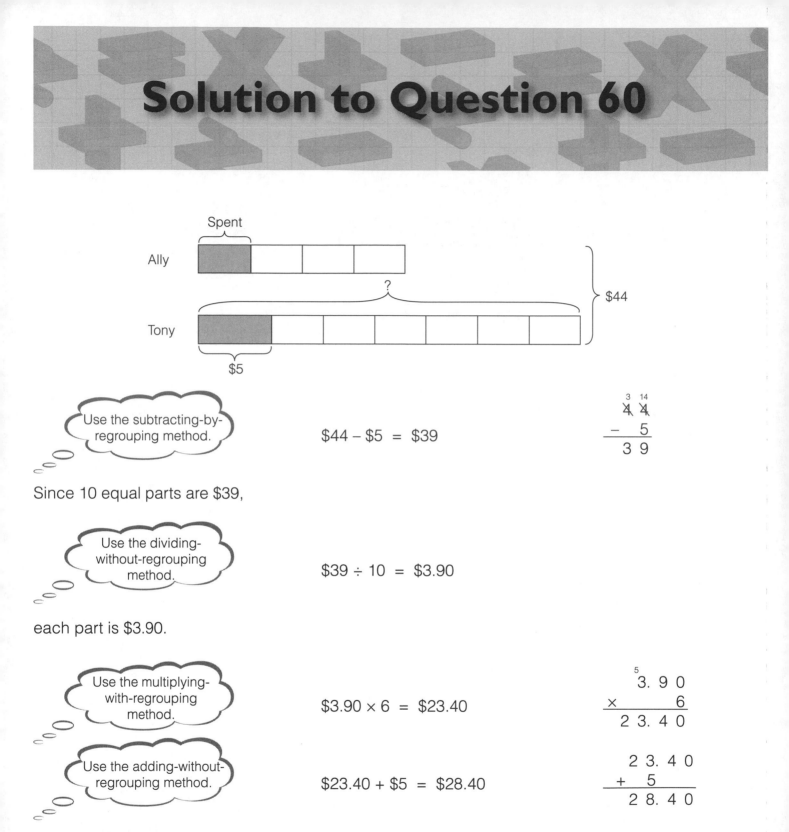

Spent

Ally

?

$44

Tony

$5

Use the subtracting-by-regrouping method.

$$\$44 - \$5 = \$39$$

$$\begin{array}{r} \overset{3}{\cancel{4}}\,\overset{14}{\cancel{4}} \\ -\quad 5 \\ \hline 3\;9 \end{array}$$

Since 10 equal parts are $39,

Use the dividing-without-regrouping method.

$$\$39 \div 10 = \$3.90$$

each part is $3.90.

Use the multiplying-with-regrouping method.

$$\$3.90 \times 6 = \$23.40$$

$$\begin{array}{r} \overset{5}{}3.\,9\,0 \\ \times \qquad 6 \\ \hline 2\,3.\,4\,0 \end{array}$$

Use the adding-without-regrouping method.

$$\$23.40 + \$5 = \$28.40$$

$$\begin{array}{r} 2\,3.\,4\,0 \\ +\quad 5 \\ \hline 2\,8.\,4\,0 \end{array}$$

Tony had **$28.40** in the beginning.

Answer: **$28.40**

Solution to Question 61

Since $\frac{1}{3}$ (or 1 part) of the money is $160,

Use the multiplying-with-regrouping method.

$$\$160 \times 2 = \$320$$

$$\begin{array}{r} {\scriptstyle 1} \\ 1\ 6\ 0 \\ \times \quad 2 \\ \hline 3\ 2\ 0 \end{array}$$

the remaining amount of money is $320.

Use the multiplication-of-fractions method.

$$\$320 \times \frac{1}{4} = \frac{\$320}{4} = \$80$$

$$\begin{array}{r} 8\ 0 \\ 4\overline{)3\ 2\ 0} \\ -3\ 2 \\ \hline 0 \\ -0 \\ \hline 0 \end{array}$$

Bridget took $80.

Use the subtracting by regrouping method.

$$\$320 - \$80 = \$240$$

$$\begin{array}{r} {\scriptstyle 2}\ {\scriptstyle 12} \\ \cancel{3}\ \cancel{2}\ 0 \\ -\quad 8\ 0 \\ \hline 2\ 4\ 0 \end{array}$$

The remaining amount of money is $240.

$$\$240 \times \frac{1}{2} = \frac{\$240}{2} = \$120$$

$$\begin{array}{r} 1\ 2\ 0 \\ 2\overline{)2\ 4\ 0} \\ -2 \\ \hline 4 \\ -4 \\ \hline 0 \\ -0 \\ \hline 0 \end{array}$$

Sasha took **$120**.

Answer: _____ **$120**

Solution to Question 62

When each boy gets 2 pieces of paper, each girl gets 3 pieces of paper. The ratio is as follows:

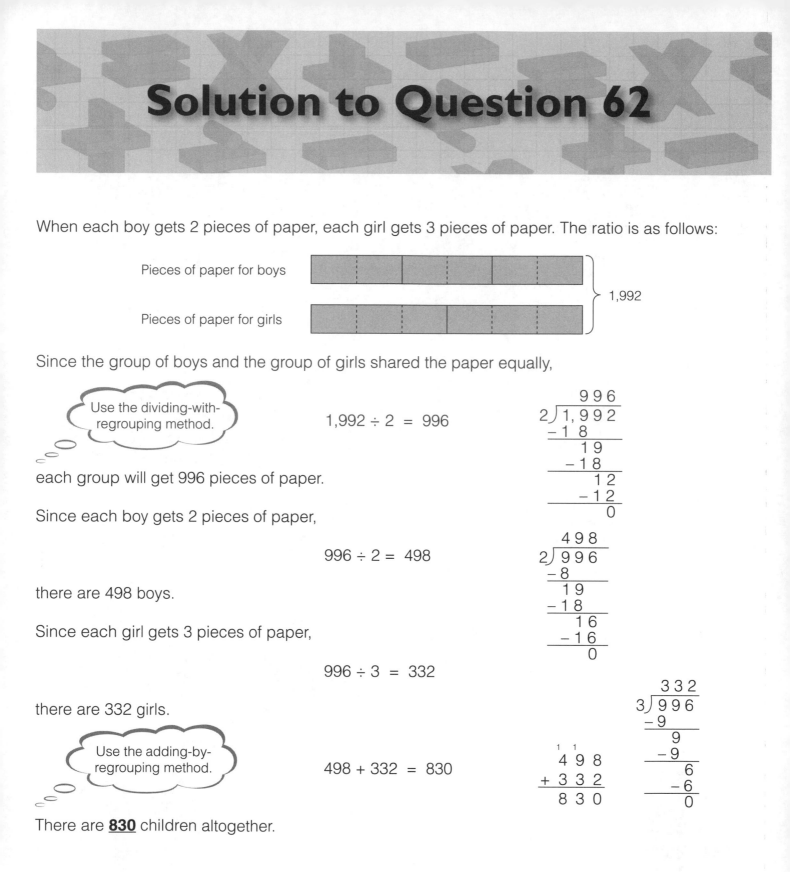

Pieces of paper for boys

Pieces of paper for girls

1,992

Since the group of boys and the group of girls shared the paper equally,

Use the dividing-with-regrouping method.

$$1,992 \div 2 = 996$$

$$\begin{array}{r} 996 \\ 2\overline{)1,992} \\ -18 \\ \hline 19 \\ -18 \\ \hline 12 \\ -12 \\ \hline 0 \end{array}$$

each group will get 996 pieces of paper.

Since each boy gets 2 pieces of paper,

$$996 \div 2 = 498$$

$$\begin{array}{r} 498 \\ 2\overline{)996} \\ -8 \\ \hline 19 \\ -18 \\ \hline 16 \\ -16 \\ \hline 0 \end{array}$$

there are 498 boys.

Since each girl gets 3 pieces of paper,

$$996 \div 3 = 332$$

there are 332 girls.

$$\begin{array}{r} 332 \\ 3\overline{)996} \\ -9 \\ \hline 9 \\ -9 \\ \hline 6 \\ -6 \\ \hline 0 \end{array}$$

Use the adding-by-regrouping method.

$$498 + 332 = 830$$

$$\begin{array}{r} {\scriptstyle 1 \ \ 1} \\ 498 \\ +332 \\ \hline 830 \end{array}$$

There are **830** children altogether.

Answer: **830 children**

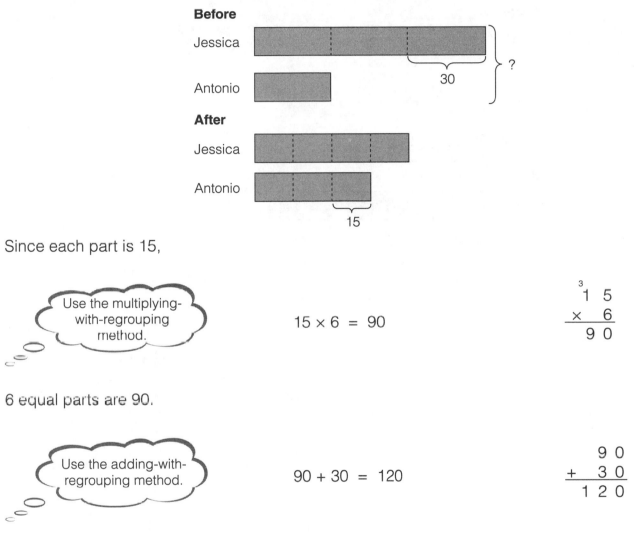

Since each part is 15,

Use the multiplying-with-regrouping method.

$15 \times 6 = 90$

$$\overset{3}{1}\ 5$$
$$\times\ \ 6$$
$$\overline{9\ 0}$$

6 equal parts are 90.

Use the adding-with-regrouping method.

$90 + 30 = 120$

$$9\ 0$$
$$+\ \ 3\ 0$$
$$\overline{1\ 2\ 0}$$

They had **120** postcards altogether in the beginning.

Answer: __**120 postcards**__

Solution to Question 64

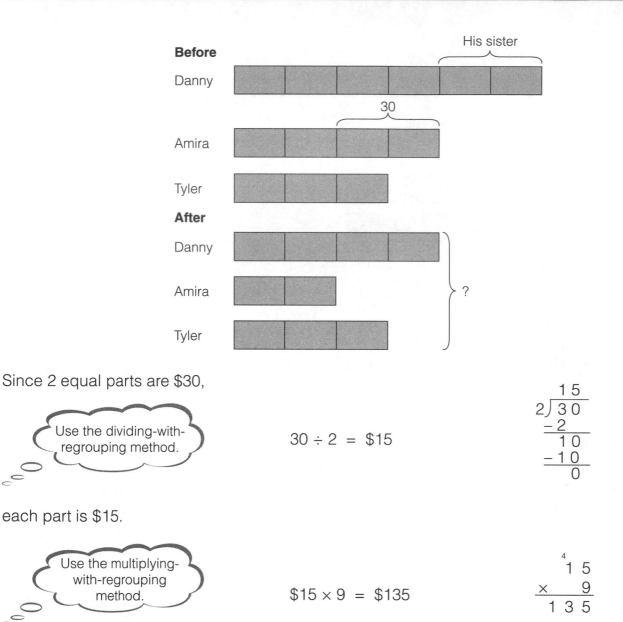

Before

His sister

Danny

30

Amira

Tyler

After

Danny

Amira

?

Tyler

Since 2 equal parts are $30,

Use the dividing-with-regrouping method.

$$30 \div 2 = \$15$$

$$\begin{array}{r} 15 \\ 2\overline{)30} \\ -2 \\ \hline 10 \\ -10 \\ \hline 0 \end{array}$$

each part is $15.

Use the multiplying-with-regrouping method.

$$\$15 \times 9 = \$135$$

$$\begin{array}{r} {}^{4}\\ 15 \\ \times 9 \\ \hline 135 \end{array}$$

They had **<u>$135</u>** left altogether.

Answer: _____ **$135**

Solution to Question 65

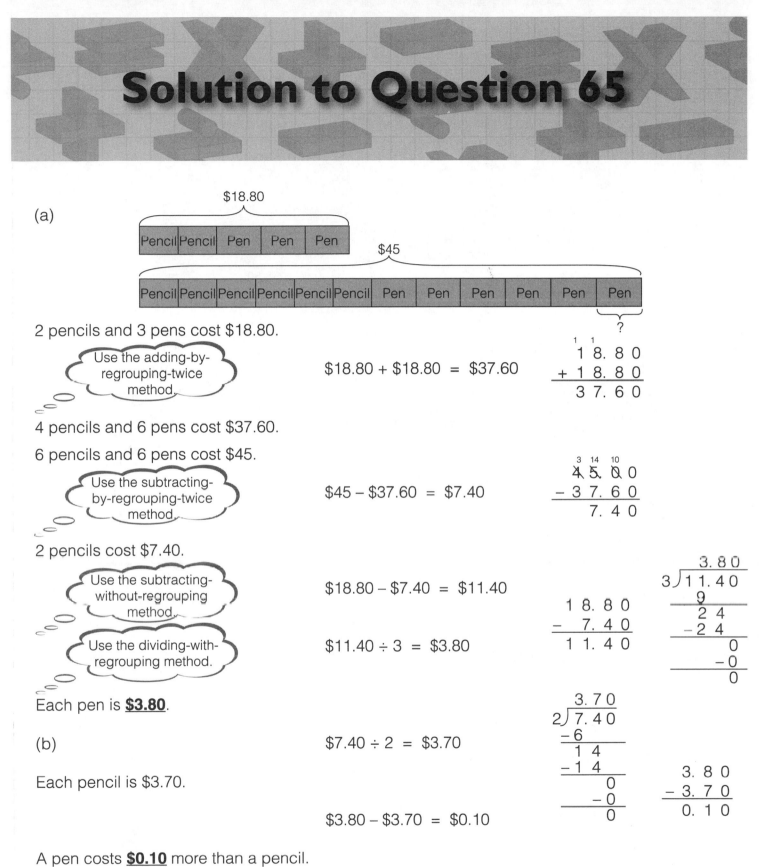

(a)

$18.80

Pencil	Pencil	Pen	Pen	Pen

$45

Pencil	Pencil	Pencil	Pencil	Pencil	Pencil	Pen	Pen	Pen	Pen	Pen	Pen

2 pencils and 3 pens cost $18.80.

Use the adding-by-regrouping-twice method.

$18.80 + $18.80 = $37.60

$$\begin{array}{r} \overset{1}{1}\,\overset{1}{8}.\ 8\ 0 \\ +\ 1\ 8.\ 8\ 0 \\ \hline 3\ 7.\ 6\ 0 \end{array}$$

4 pencils and 6 pens cost $37.60.

6 pencils and 6 pens cost $45.

Use the subtracting-by-regrouping-twice method.

$45 − $37.60 = $7.40

$$\begin{array}{r} \overset{3}{\cancel4}\,\overset{14}{\cancel5}.\ \overset{10}{\cancel0}\ 0 \\ -\ 3\ 7.\ 6\ 0 \\ \hline 7.\ 4\ 0 \end{array}$$

2 pencils cost $7.40.

Use the subtracting-without-regrouping method.

$18.80 − $7.40 = $11.40

Use the dividing-with-regrouping method.

$11.40 ÷ 3 = $3.80

$$\begin{array}{r} 1\ 8.\ 8\ 0 \\ -\ \ \ 7.\ 4\ 0 \\ \hline 1\ 1.\ 4\ 0 \end{array}$$

$$\begin{array}{r} 3.8\,0 \\ 3\overline{)1\,1.4\,0} \\ \underline{9} \\ 2\,4 \\ \underline{-2\,4} \\ 0 \\ \underline{-\ 0} \\ 0 \end{array}$$

Each pen is **$3.80**.

(b)

$7.40 ÷ 2 = $3.70

Each pencil is $3.70.

$3.80 − $3.70 = $0.10

$$\begin{array}{r} 3.7\,0 \\ 2\overline{)7.4\,0} \\ \underline{-6} \\ 1\,4 \\ \underline{-1\,4} \\ 0 \\ \underline{-\ 0} \\ 0 \end{array}$$

$$\begin{array}{r} 3.\ 8\ 0 \\ -\ 3.\ 7\ 0 \\ \hline 0.\ 1\ 0 \end{array}$$

A pen costs **$0.10** more than a pencil.

Answer: (a) <u>**$3.80**</u>

(b) <u>**$0.10 more**</u>

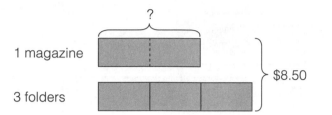

1 magazine

3 folders

?

$8.50

Since 5 equal parts are $8.50,

Use the dividing-with-regrouping method.

$8.50 ÷ 5 = $1.70

$$\begin{array}{r} 1.\,7\,0 \\ 5\overline{)\,8.\,5\,0} \\ -5 \\ \hline 3\,5 \\ -3\,5 \\ \hline 0 \\ -0 \\ \hline 0 \end{array}$$

each part is $1.70.

Use the multiplying-with-regrouping method.

$1.70 × 2 = $3.40

$$\begin{array}{r} ^{1}\,1.\,7\,0 \\ \times\,2 \\ \hline 3.\,4\,0 \end{array}$$

The price of the magazine was **$3.40**.

Answer: _____**$3.40**_____

Use the adding-without-regrouping method.

$58 + $30 = $88

$$\begin{array}{r} 5\ 8 \\ +\ 3\ 0 \\ \hline 8\ 8 \end{array}$$

A pair of Brand A and Brand B watches costs $88.

Use the dividing-with-regrouping method.

$22,000 ÷ $88 = 250

$$\begin{array}{r} 250 \\ 88\overline{)22,000} \\ -176 \\ \hline 440 \\ -440 \\ \hline 0 \\ -0 \\ \hline 0 \end{array}$$

250 pairs of watches cost $22,000.

Use the multiplying-with-regrouping method.

250 × 2 = 500

$$\begin{array}{r} ^{1}2\ 5\ 0 \\ \times\ \ \ \ \ 2 \\ \hline 5\ 0\ 0 \end{array}$$

There are **500** watches.

Answer: **500 watches**

Solution to Question 68

Use the multiplication-of-fractions method.

$\frac{1}{7} \times 14 = 2$

2 equal parts are women.

28,000

| | | | | | | | | | | | | | |

Men   Women   Children

Since 14 equal parts are 28,000,

Use the dividing-with-regrouping method.

$28,000 \div 14 = 2,000$

each part is 2,000.

$$
\begin{array}{r}
2,000 \\
14 \overline{)28,000} \\
\underline{-28} \\
0 \\
\underline{-0} \\
0 \\
\underline{-0} \\
0 \\
\underline{-0} \\
0
\end{array}
$$

Use the multiplying-without-regrouping method.

$3 \times 2,000 = 6,000$

$$
\begin{array}{r}
2,000 \\
\times \quad\quad 3 \\
\hline
6,000
\end{array}
$$

There were 6,000 children.

Use the subtraction-of-fractions method.

$1 - \frac{3}{4} = \frac{4}{4} - \frac{3}{4} = \frac{1}{4}$

$$
\begin{array}{r}
1,500 \\
4 \overline{)6,000} \\
\underline{-4} \\
20 \\
\underline{-20} \\
0 \\
\underline{-0} \\
0 \\
\underline{-0} \\
0
\end{array}
$$

$\frac{1}{4}$ of the children were girls.

Use the multiplication-of-fractions method.

$\frac{1}{4} \times 6,000 = \frac{6,000}{4} = 1,500$

There were **1,500** girls.

Answer: **1,500 girls**

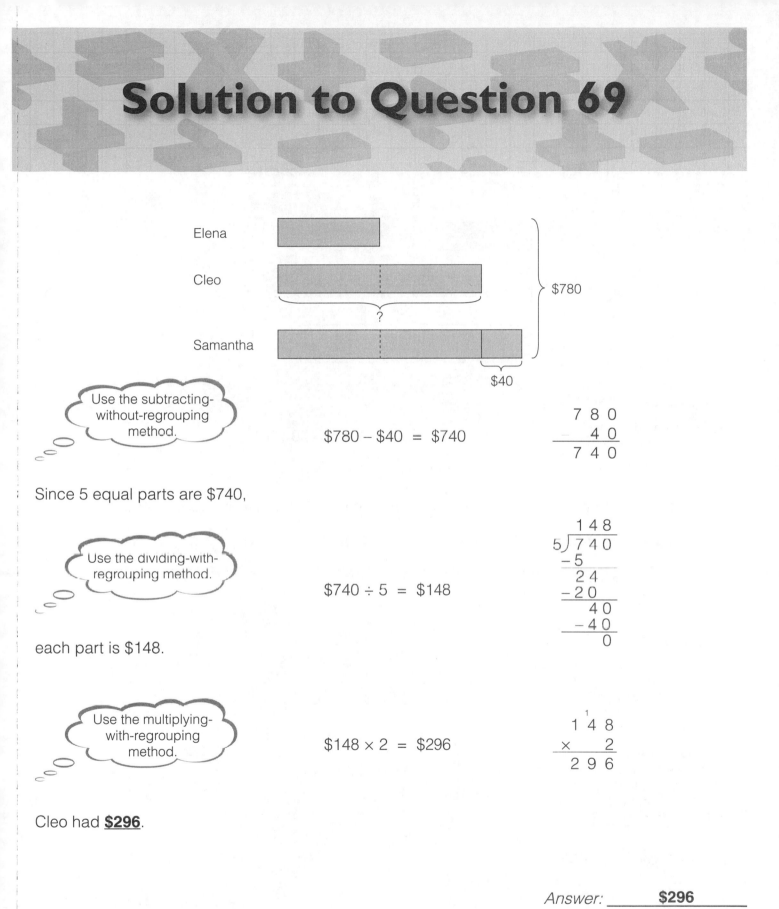

Elena

Cleo

Samantha

$780

$40

Use the subtracting-without-regrouping method.

$780 – $40 = $740

$$\begin{array}{r} 7\ 8\ 0 \\ -\quad 4\ 0 \\ \hline 7\ 4\ 0 \end{array}$$

Since 5 equal parts are $740,

Use the dividing-with-regrouping method.

$740 ÷ 5 = $148

$$\begin{array}{r} 1\ 4\ 8 \\ 5\overline{)7\ 4\ 0} \\ -5 \\ \hline 2\ 4 \\ -2\ 0 \\ \hline 4\ 0 \\ -4\ 0 \\ \hline 0 \end{array}$$

each part is $148.

Use the multiplying-with-regrouping method.

$148 × 2 = $296

$$\begin{array}{r} 1\overset{1}{4}\ 8 \\ \times\quad\ \ 2 \\ \hline 2\ 9\ 6 \end{array}$$

Cleo had **$296**.

Answer: _____ **$296**

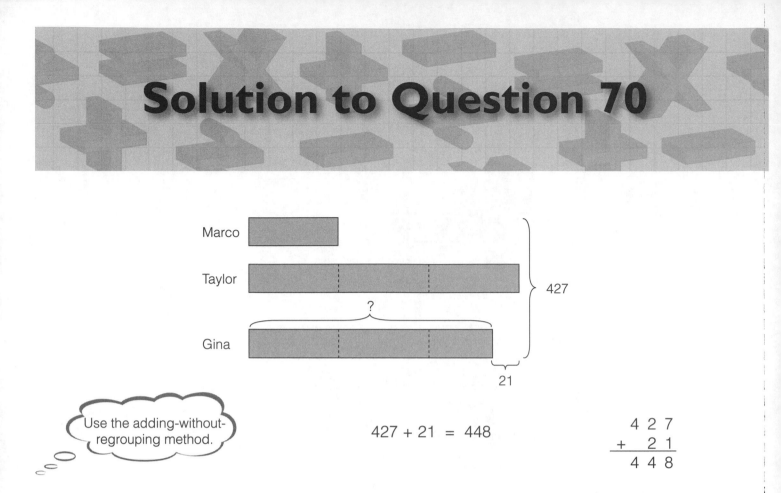

Use the adding-without-regrouping method.

$$427 + 21 = 448$$

```
  4 2 7
+   2 1
-------
  4 4 8
```

They would have 448 pebbles altogether if Gina had the same number of pebbles as Taylor.

Use the dividing-with-regrouping method.

$$448 ÷ 7 = 64$$

```
      6 4
   -------
 7 ) 4 4 8
    -4 2
    -----
      2 8
    - 2 8
    -----
        0
```

Each part is 64.

Use the multiplying-with-regrouping method.

$$64 × 3 = 192$$

```
    ¹
    6 4
  ×   3
  -----
  1 9 2
```

Use the subtracting-without-regrouping method.

$$192 - 21 = 171$$

```
  1 9 2
-   2 1
-------
  1 7 1
```

Gina collected **171** pebbles.

Answer: **171 pebbles**

Notes

Notes

Notes

Notes

Notes

Notes

Notes

Notes